Women
of Faith

by Donna Kafer

Bridge-Logos
Alachua, FL 32615 USA

Bridge-Logos

Alachua, FL 32615 USA

Women of Faith
by Donna Kafer

Copyright ©2008 by Bridge-Logos

Printed in Canada.

Library of Congress Catalog Card Number: 2008927492
ISBN: 978-0-88270-478-4

Unless otherwise noted, all Scripture notations are taken from the *King James Version* (KJV) of the Bible.

G1.316.N.m806.35240

Dedication

To My Maternal Grandmother, Alverta Reynolds Hamilton

In memory of the love you gave so freely, for taking me along to church and for sharing your love of Jesus Christ with me. It was your inspiring, never failing faith that encouraged me to never give up.

To My Paternal Grandmother, Aldyth Baardson Andersen

In memory of your steadfast faith and the loving care you gave in serving your husband, children, and grandchildren. Thank you for believing in me as a writer and as a woman loved by God.

Contents

Faith of Our Mothers

Faith of Martyrs and Saints

Faith of Poets, Writers, and Composers

Acknowledgments

In the summer of 2006 I met a warm, witty man by the name of Guy Morrell, and the door into the realm of publishing at last opened for me. I had long dreamed of having a book in print, and now I had the opportunity. In May 2007, when my first book, *Women of Courage,* was soon to be released, I received the call that Guy Morrell had died in his sleep. I had such a mixture of emotions—shock, sadness, and personal loss—for he had been somewhat of a mentor to me as we had discussed and envisioned future books.

Yet I reasoned that I really did not know Guy that well, so, why the sadness? I realized that Guy had blessed me with the opportunity to not only write, but to let hundreds, if not thousands, of readers know my thoughts and read my writing on great Christian women. What a blessed gift indeed. Guy Morrell was instrumental in my becoming an author, so I will be forever grateful for his kindness in enabling me to make a difference in the world for Christ.

I would like to thank Wendy Wood, my editor, for her tireless, dedicated work in tidying up my manuscript. Her loving suggestions and ongoing friendship inspire me to be a better writer. Wendy is an absolute treasure and a great woman of faith.

Finally, without the beautiful flowers and other graphics in these pages, this book would not be the lovely, creative work that it is. Elizabeth Nason is a tremendous graphic designer and her work in this book and in *Women of Courage* has touched many people in a profound way. Thank you, Elizabeth, for capturing the beauty of the flowers that represent the women in these pages and for being a true woman of faith.

PART ONE

Faith

of Our

Mothers

Introduction to
Part One

Faith of Our Mothers

One cannot argue that mothers are and will forevermore be linked to enduring remembrances of comfort and safety. In all of our collective thoughts we, who were so blessed to have mothers who lovingly cared for us through our early years, hold these memories most dear.

If not for the nurturing, character-shaping role of mother, where would we all be? Most who are mothers long to be the type of parent that instills fond memories in their children. We want that fuzzy warm feeling to be there with our daughters and sons when they go away from home and hopefully remember that Mom was always there for them.

We all strive to be the mom that can do it all. From baking the best cookies that our third grader's class has ever tasted, to having the coolest home that all our teenager's friends want to hang out at. We want to be *that* mom!

It does seem that no matter how hard we try we still come up short and feel somewhat disappointed in ourselves as mothers. We try so hard to be the best at what we really do believe is the most important job in the world. How can we, who believe in Jesus Christ as Lord and Savior, be the type of godly mom we want to be?

The Bible says that children are a gift from the Lord (Psalm 127:3-5). When we receive a gift we are joyful, elated and hold close that which was received as a blessing. The Greek word for this type of mother-love is *phileoteknos* and appears in Titus 2:4 and speaks to our understanding that this type of love is one of affectionately embracing and nurturing. It means that we instinctively prefer our offspring, tenderly caring for and meeting their needs. God designed us to be this way with our children, teaching and guiding them with all of our hearts.

I came to motherhood later in life and had always prayed that God would bless me with a child of my own. When I realized that I would never have a child of my own, a baby to hold in my aching arms, I resigned myself to never experiencing being a "mom." But when I was unexpectedly presented with the opportunity to adopt a newborn through a private adoption, I was ecstatic! What unparalleled joy at the prospect of having a child of my own. I met the young mother when she was only four months pregnant and was so thrilled to know this human being that was so willing to place her unborn child with me— a gift from one to another. I was in the delivery room when my daughter, Andrea Elizabeth, was born, and I felt a rush of love from every fiber of my being for her, my baby, my daughter, my gift from God.

I share this for those who are adopted or are an adoptive parent, so that you might be reassured that this is a truly natural birth process for you. Adoption is a highly favorable way for a family to be established. Remember that our Father in Heaven adopted us as well, so that we are now heirs along with Jesus Christ our Lord.

As a mother we are commanded to parent a child in several ways through God's Holy Word. We are to be available morning, noon, and night (Deuteronomy 6:6-7) and be involved in all their daily activities (Ephesians 6:4). It can be a challenge for those of us who work outside the home and are extra busy in this day and age, but it can be done. We just take every opportunity to interact with our kids and share our Christian values and beliefs with them as it pertains to their lives.

We are called to teach, train and discipline our children (Ephesians 6:4; Hebrews 12:5-11; Proverbs 13:24, 19:18, 22:15, 23:13-14, 22:6, 29:15-17). Teaching our children comes as we interact and live out the godly life as we instruct them to live. We can train them to have compassion, to be nurturers, to care about others because God first loved us (1 John 4:19). Disciplining our sons and daughters means to set healthy boundaries and constructive and firm guidelines for their protection and well-being. Discipline actually gives them confidence in life, freeing them from the incredible fear of being out of control and in danger. Having boundaries gives them a sense of safety and relieves them from feeling that they have to be the adult in scary situations.

We are our children's champions, advocates and cheerleaders. We are the major influence on the way they see the world and how they react to it and interact in it. Be of good cheer, Mom; God is guiding you as you make your way in this role in your dear one's life. He is the parent who loves you, guides you and helps you in your decision-making process concerning that son or daughter. Trust Him for their lives, because they are gifts from Him, and you will ultimately release them into the world. As we all are, they are God's, so when they someday stand before Him they will not have you by their side.

When our children accept Jesus and embrace the Christian faith we who are mothers rejoice. We, along with the heavenly host, celebrate and sing with gratefulness that the ones we cherish above all things on earth now know the grace that will give them eternal life. Such joy knows no bounds and is unprecedented in all of the earth. In Isaiah 49:15 it says, "Can a mother forget the baby at her breast and have no compassion on the child she has borne?" It is this joy that fills our hearts as mothers, this little babe whom we worried over, cried over, and spent endless hours in the darkness of night over, is now saved and will live forevermore in the kingdom of God. There is nothing finer.

In the following pages are seven stories of mothers who sacrificed much, who gave their all, and endured everything to lead their children into the saving grace of Almighty God. May their stories encourage, inspire and illuminate us.

THE MADONNA LILY OPENS ITS PETALS TO THE MORNING SUN IN
RADIANT OBEDIENCE. PRECIOUS AND PURE OF HEART, LIKE THE GLORIOUS
DISPLAY OF THE LILY, IS MARY, DEAR MOTHER OF JESUS. THE LILY YIELDS
ITS BEAUTY TO GLORIFY THE CREATOR. SUCH WAS THE LIFE OF MARY—
OBEDIENT, YIELDING AND GLORIOUS.

Mary

The Mother of Jesus

From the time we were little children curled on our mother's lap listening to the nativity story, we so easily pictured the family: dutiful Joseph, the baby Jesus asleep in the hay and his doting mother, Mary. She was so sweet, so innocent, that it was easy to picture her in our hearts and minds. When we sang "Silent Night" or "Away in a Manger," we felt sad that there was no room for her and Joseph at the inn and that the poor baby Jesus had no where to lay his sweet head. The Christmas story invoked many feelings within our hearts, feelings of concern for the little family, feelings of excitement when the angels appeared to the shepherds with tidings of joy. But the greatest feeling of all was the wonder of the power of God to make Christmas happen at all.

It is easy to envision Mary holding the baby, her eyes lingering tenderly on His dear face. We have all marveled at the willingness of this young maiden to be used of God in such a magnificent way, to be obedient in surrendering her will to the Lord and carrying in her womb the Savior of the world. Did she really understand the profound reality of this blessing on her life? Did she truly know that the promised Messiah was being born into the world through her?

Luke 1:26-38 tells how the angel Gabriel appears to her announcing :"Greetings, you who are highly favored! The Lord is with you." The Scriptures say that she was greatly troubled by this greeting and wondered what kind of message this might possibly be. The angel tells her not to be afraid because God has found favor in her, and she will be with child and give birth to a son that she will name Jesus. Gabriel also tells her that, "The Lord God will give him the throne of his father David and he will reign over the house of Jacob forever; his kingdom will never end."

She could have responded in all manner of ways to this thrilling message of a son that would rule forever, but what does this young girl fixate on? Being pregnant!

"How will this be," Mary asked the angel, "since I am a virgin?" Her mind must have been racing, her heart fluttering with this strange pronouncement over her life.

Once again the angel reassures her: "The Holy Spirit will come upon you, and the power of the Most High will overshadow you. So the holy one to be born will be called the Son of God" (Luke 1:34). To further astonish her, Gabriel declares that her relative Elizabeth is going to have a child in her old age, and she who was said to be barren is in her sixth month. For nothing is impossible with God.

Mary's immediate response to the angel's final proclamation is heart warming and inspiring: "I am the Lord's servant, may it be to me as you have said." Then the angel left her.

It was at this time that Mary decided to visit her cousin Elizabeth who was living with her husband Zechariah in a town that was a considerable distance away. From her home in Nazareth she would have had to travel about one hundred miles to an area known as Juttah in the neighborhood of Maon, mentioned in Joshua 15:55; 21:16.

It was in this hill country of Judah that we hear the blessing that would resound through the ages. When Mary entered her cousin's house and called out her greeting, the babe in Elizabeth's womb leapt and she was filled with the Holy Spirit. In a loud voice she exclaimed:

> "Blessed are you among women, and blessed is the child you will bear! But why am I so favored, that the mother of my Lord should come to me? As soon as the sound of your greeting reached my ears, the baby in my womb leaped for joy. Blessed is she who has believed that what the Lord has said to her will be accomplished" (Luke 1:42-45).

"Blessed is she who has believed that what the Lord has said to her will be accomplished." What grand faith indeed! I pray to have faith like Mary AND Elizabeth. Lord, help me to recognize your power over the elements of science, for you are the Master Creator and Designer, and what you will to happen WILL happen!

Mary's Song

And Mary said:

"My soul glorifies the Lord and my spirit rejoices in God my Savior, for he has been mindful of the humble state of his servant. From now on all generations will call me blessed, for the Mighty One has done great things for me—holy is his name.

"His mercy extends to those who fear him from generation to generation. He has performed mighty deeds with his arm, he has scattered those who are proud in their inmost thoughts. He has brought down rulers from their thrones, but has lifted up the humble. He has filled the hungry with good things but has sent the rich away empty.

"He has helped his servant Israel remembering to be merciful, to Abraham and his descendants forever, even as he said to our fathers."

Notice all the lovely things that welled out of her tender spirit as she thanked and worshipped her Lord before others. Mary recognized her status as a lowly, poor servant of the Most High God, but also rejoiced that she will be remembered as being chosen and blessed for all time. Not only did God bless her, but Israel, and all of Abraham's descendents forever and ever.

Joseph, her betrothed, had experienced a supernatural event concerning Mary's pregnancy. In a dream an angel of the Lord appeared to him and said: "Joseph son of David, do not be afraid to take Mary home as your wife, because what is conceived in her is from the Holy Spirit. She will give birth to a son, and you are to give him the name Jesus, because he will save his people from their sins." All this took place to fulfill what the Lord had said through the prophet. "The virgin will be with child and will give birth to a son, and they will call him Immanuel, which means, 'God with us.'"

When Mary and Joseph traveled to Bethlehem to register for the Roman census, she was nearing the time of the impending birth of her baby. Every man was ordered to the city of his fathers to register for the census, and for Joseph, Bethlehem was this very place. This was to fulfill the prophecy recorded in Micah 5:2 concerning where the Messiah was to be born: "You, O Bethlehem, are only a small village in Judah. Yet a ruler of Israel will come from you, one whose origins are from the distant past." The prophecies of the past were being fulfilled through the power of the Holy Spirit and the obedience of the two young people committed to serving their God.

In Isaiah 7:14-15 it says:

"The Lord will choose the sign. Look! The virgin will conceive a baby! She will give birth to a son and will call him Immanuel—meaning 'God is with us.' By the time this child is old enough to eat curds and honey he will know enough to choose what is right and reject what is wrong."

And again in Isaiah 9: 6-7:

"A child is born to us, a son is given to us. The government will rest on His shoulders. These will be his royal titles: Wonderful Counselor, Mighty God, Everlasting Father, Prince of Peace. His ever increasing, peaceful government will never end. He will rule with fairness and justice from the throne of his ancestor David."

The commitment of the LORD Almighty will guarantee this! These prophecies were made some 700 years before the angel Gabriel appeared to Mary with his message of God's plan for her and mankind. How could she ever have imagined that she would be a part of something so magnificent and earth shaking?

Luke, chapter 2 tells us how Mary and Joseph could not find a place to stay when they arrived in Bethlehem. It must have been very scary for them when Mary went into labor and there was no place for them to prepare for their child's entry into the world. But they were able to take shelter in a place where the animals were kept, and there Mary gave birth to her firstborn, a son, our Jesus. It says she wrapped Him and swaddled Him in cloths and laid Him in a manger, for there was no room for them in the inn (Luke 2:7).

Mary must have been exhausted after the birth. As she lay with the babe at her breast, reveling in his delicate features and the wonder of Him, shepherds appeared from the fields where they had been tending their sheep. A glorious host of angels told them of the baby's birth and that they would find him lying in a manger. They came and saw Mary, Joseph and the baby, just as they had been told by the angels. They told everything that had happened in the fields that night and what they heard from the angels, who praised God by saying: "Glory to God in the highest, and on earth peace to men on whom his favor rests." Mary treasured up all these things and pondered them in her heart.

According to the Law of Moses a male child was circumcised on the eighth day after his birth. It was during this time that Mary and Joseph named their son Jesus, just as they were instructed by the angel. The baby then would have been presented to God in the temple, his parents acknowledging that

He belonged to God. The child would be "redeemed," that is repurchased, by giving a sacrificial offering in his place. (Exodus 13:2-16). This was done after the purification of the mother. For forty days following the birth of a son—eighty days for a daughter—a mother was considered unclean. At the end of this ritual impurity, a sacrifice was offered as part of her cleansing process. Mary and Joseph did all of this in an orderly, reverent way, according to the Law of Moses.

> When all of their purification requirements had been met, they brought their son to Jerusalem. Their hearts were in one accord as they obediently kept the instruction of the Law: every firstborn male is to be consecrated to the Lord and to offer a sacrifice in keeping with what is said in the Law of the Lord: "a pair of doves or two young pigeons."
> Now there was a man in Jerusalem called Simeon who was righteous and devout. He was waiting for the consolation of Israel, and the Holy Spirit was upon him. It had been revealed to him by the Holy Spirit that he would not die before he had seen the Lord's Christ. Moved by the Spirit, he went into the temple courts. When the parents brought in the child Jesus to do for him what the custom of the Law required, Simeon took him in his arms and praised God, saying: "Sovereign Lord, as you have promised, you now dismiss your servant in peace. For my eyes have seen your salvation, which you have prepared in the sight of all people, a light for revelation to the Gentiles and for glory to your people Israel." (Luke 2:25-32)

I wonder if Mary hesitated when they were approached by the old man, Simeon, before she placed her precious bundle in his arms. But upon hearing his praise to God concerning their child, both Mary and Joseph marveled at what was said about

Him. Then Simeon blessed them and said to Mary, His mother: "This child is destined to cause the falling and rising of many in Israel and to be a sign that will be spoken against, so that the thoughts of many hearts will be revealed. And a sword will pierce your own soul too" (Luke 2:35).

At the last statement, "And a sword will pierce your own soul too," do you wonder if she might have caught her breath, her eyes misting slightly as she gazed on the innocent face of the babe held so reverently in this stranger's arms. She might have anxiously searched the deep crevices that lined the face of the prophet, puzzling over this last piece of his blessing. How could this tiny blessing, so perfect, so sweet, ever cause her heart any anguish or trouble? And what of all the tremendous promises that were being told about His future? Surely, her son was destined for greatness and wondrous authority. Mary's concern was probably fleeting as she and Joseph continued to marvel at everything that was being told to them about their precious baby.

At the same moment that Simeon was blessing the baby, they were approached by an old prophetess by the name of Anna, the daughter of Phanuel, of the tribe of Asher. This devoted woman of God had been widowed for quite a very long time, having been married a mere seven years when her husband died. It says in the scriptures that Anna stayed in the temple night and day, worshipping, fasting and praying to the Lord. Anna gave thanks to God and spoke about the child to all who were looking forward to the redemption of Jerusalem (Luke 2: 36-38). Luke 2:39 says that after the sacrifices were completed, Joseph, Mary and the baby returned to Nazareth.

But what happened to the wise men? Matthew's gospel account doesn't specify how long it was after Jesus' birth that the wise men arrived in Jerusalem following a star that they had seen in the East (Matthew 2:1-2). As little children we grew up believing that the wise men were at the manger the night of Jesus' birth. The nativity crèche displays at Christmas always showed the wise men present at the manger, with their camels and their gifts. When King Herod listened to these strangers seeking a new king, he called the chief priests and asked for their scripture reference. Upon hearing the prophecy concerning where the child would be born, he sent the wise men to Bethlehem. He told them to report back to him so he might worship the babe too.

Bethlehem is only five miles from Jerusalem and when the wise men left King Herod they immediately looked to the heavens to see exactly where the star would lead them. Their only concern was for the quest they were on, not King Herod's edict. The scriptures tell us that the wise men looked to the star to see where the child was abiding. It does not say that they went to Bethlehem at all, but rather the star showed them where Jesus would be found. And that was in Nazareth. (Look again at Luke 2:39.)

When the wise men left the young family, they were instructed by God not to return to King Herod (Matthew 2:12), so they charted their long journey home away from Jerusalem. It was then that God instructed Joseph in a dream to flee into Egypt with the child and his mother, for Herod would seek his life (Matthew 2:13). Herod, realizing that he had been deceived, issued an edict ordering that all male children, age two and under, in Bethlehem and its districts be put to death (Matthew 2:16). He understood the time frame of when the star first appeared and even considered the fact that Jesus might not have been in Bethlehem any longer. This is why he extended his search to include regions surrounding Bethlehem as well, intent on killing this challenger to his throne.

Mary's heart must have felt the very first pangs of fear for her son during this time. An alarmed Joseph had awakened her, telling her of his dream to get up and go into Egypt. Already her son was being threatened, so imagine her fears for the future well-being of her firstborn. But because of Joseph's immediate obedience in all things, the life of Jesus was spared from the sword of Herod's soldiers.

After King Herod's death God told Joseph that it was safe to return to their land with Mary and Jesus. With God's continued guidance the three from Galilee traveled back to their home and family in Nazareth. After this we hear nothing more about the home life of the family except for the Scripture in Luke 2:40—that the child grew and became strong: He was filled with wisdom and the grace of God was upon Him.

The next we hear of the boy Jesus was when the family traveled together to Jerusalem for the Feast of the Passover. He was twelve years old at the time, and it must have been very exciting for Him to travel with His mother, father and other relatives to be a part of such a wonderful celebration. It is the return journey home that is recorded for us to try and understand.

In Luke 2:43 it says:

> After the feast was over, while his parents were returning home, Jesus stayed behind in Jerusalem, but they were unaware of it. Thinking he was in their company, they traveled on for a day, when they began looking for him. After three days they found him in the temple courts, sitting among the teachers, listening to them and asking them questions. Everyone who heard him was amazed at his understanding and his answers. When his parents saw him, they were astonished.

His mother said to him, "son, why have you treated us like this? Your father and I have been anxiously searching for you."

"Why were you searching for me? He asked. "Didn't you know I had to be in my Father's house?"

But they did not understand what he was saying to them. Then he went down to Nazareth with them and was obedient to them. But his mother treasured all these things in her heart. And Jesus grew in wisdom and stature, and in favor with God and men.

Soon after Jesus' ministry began at the age of thirty, we read about Mary's understanding of what He was able to do. Her confidence in Him was evident when she compelled Him to turn water into wine—His first miracle. We know that Jesus' ministry began to draw attention to what He was doing, healing the people, feeding the hungry, and most of all giving hope to the hopeless.

Then there came the night that Mary's son would be arrested in the Garden of Gethsemane by the Roman soldiers. Do you suppose she was awakened in the night and told the frightening news concerning her son? Her mind must have tried to grapple with the unfolding facts, His betrayal by one of His own and the plot of the Pharisees to charge Him with heresy.

Jesus was scourged by the centurions, beaten beyond recognition. And then Mary's son, her innocent son was sentenced to death. The tears must have stung her eyes bitterly as she realized her child was being taken from her in such a savage, brutal way. Her heart was being torn asunder and there was nothing that she could do about it—absolutely nothing.

Once at Golgotha with John by her side, Mary watched in horror as the Roman guards drove nails into her son's hands and feet, all the while mocking and calling Him names. They had put a crown of thorns on His head and the blood ran down His beaten face in rivulets. When they lifted Him on the cross, she heard His agonizing groan as the cross settled into the ground where it would stand for all to witness as He suffered. Pontius Pilate had ordered a sign hung on the top of the cross stating that this was the King of the Jews.

Near the cross of Jesus stood his mother, his mother's sister, Mary the wife of Clopas, and Mary Magdalene. When Jesus saw his mother there and the disciple whom he loved standing nearby, he said to his mother, "Dear woman, here is your son," and to the disciple, "Here is your mother." From that time on, this disciple took her into his home (John 19:25-27).

Perhaps it was here that Mary must have recalled the old prophet Simeon's prophecy that "her heart would be pierced." Her heart was indeed pierced as she stood at the foot of the cross watching as Jesus' life blood slipped away from Him. Her son, her beloved child that she had cherished and raised was being torn from her, taken in such an evil, malevolent manner.

When Jesus cried out, "It is finished," and gave up his Spirit to God, the heavens darkened and the earth shook violently. Mary must have been shaken to her very core by these events, held in the sheltering arms of John, protected from the elements and the intensifying moment.

The very last we hear about Jesus' mother is in the book of Acts in the upper room. It was here that we see that she was included in the group of people prayerfully waiting for the gift that Jesus promised. Before He had ascended to Heaven He told them, "Do not leave Jerusalem, but wait for the gift my father promised, which you have heard me speak about. For

John baptized with water, but in a few days you will be baptized with the Holy Spirit" (Acts 1: 4-5).

"They all joined together constantly in prayer, along with the women and Mary, the mother of Jesus and with his brothers" (Acts 1:12-14).

Mary, mother of Jesus is an example of obedience to God. She will always thrill our hearts with the perfect image of motherhood. Her tender mercies, devoted dedication, and willingness to serve captures our imaginations. Hebrews 11:6 says, "And without faith it is impossible to please God, because anyone who comes to him must believe that he exists and that he rewards those who earnestly seek him."

Scripture Application

"MY SOUL GLORIFIES THE LORD
AND MY SPIRIT REJOICES IN
GOD MY SAVIOR, FOR HE HAS
BEEN MINDFUL AT THE HUMBLE
STATE OF HIS SERVANT. FROM
NOW ON ALL GENERATIONS
WILL CALL ME BLESSED."

LUKE 1: 46-48

Reflections on Faithful Obedience

Think of Mary's obedience in her situation. How would you have responded to the angel Gabriel's message?

Have you ever been in a situation that required your careful obedience, even if it was uncomfortable?

Think about how you would respond to God today if He called on you to be obedient in such a life-altering way. What would be your answer?

THE MOTHER'S TEARS FLOWER SYMBOLIZES THE KIND OF LOVING,
PRAYING MOTHER ST. MONICA WAS. HER SOFT TEARS NEVER CEASED
TO FLOW FOR HER CHILD. PRECIOUS MONICA WHOSE LOVE KNEW NO
BOUNDS FOR A CHILD THAT WOULD NOT SURRENDER TO THE SAVIOR,
YOUR COURAGE INSPIRES US TO NEVER GIVE UP.

Saint Monica

A.D. 333 – A.D. 387

Mother of St. Augustine

For those of us who have had a praying mother or grandmother who sought the Lord on our behalf, we can respond to St. Monica with a sigh of understanding. To have your son or daughter brought alive and well into the Kingdom of God is the greatest answer to prayer for any brokenhearted Christian mother. There is indeed hope for all the sons and daughters of the world who have a praying mother interceding for them.

Monica, the mother of Saint Augustine was just such a mother. Much is recorded in history by her once wayward son, and it is by his writings that we know just how much she loved him and interceded for his salvation. His enduring gratitude to his mother for leading him to the Savior of the world speaks through his confessions.

A holy bishop who became exasperated by St. Monica's prayers on behalf of her son spoke these prophetic and immortal words: "It is impossible that a child of such tears should perish." Her single-minded determination in freeing her sinful son from his heretical lifestyle became the hallmark for her sanctity and for her son's confessions of her mighty faith to the world. His mother's faith at the throne of Almighty God drew him into the presence of the power of the Holy Spirit. Augustine could not resist the love of God invading his life and the only thing he could do was embrace the faith of his mother.

St. Monica was born into a deeply devout Catholic family in Roman North Africa near Carthage, perhaps around 333 A.D. Growing up in such a pious family, everyone in the household was expected to behave in a virtuous manner. With the help of a strict servant woman, Monica was raised to conform to Christian moral teachings in order that she might grow into responsible Christian adulthood. One interesting story of a minor slip in her Christian devotion came about as the result of her fondness for wine as a girl. Another young girl, a slave, taunted her on one occasion for drunkenness, and she was so ashamed that she vowed not to drink thereafter.

You would think that Monica's prospects in marriage would be to some upright, pious Christian. But she marries a pagan by the name of Patricius, who is an official in their town of Thagaste. It is reported that her husband had a hot temper and was repeatedly unfaithful to her but never verbally or physically abused her. His mother was not much better, being of like disposition, so husband and mother-in-law caused dear Monica much unhappiness.

It was Monica's habit of prayer and service to others that caused her husband so much annoyance, but ironically it was her love for the Lord and her fellow man that actually caused him to hold her in a sort of reverence. Monica's marriage wasn't the only unhappy union in their native town. So among the other wives and mothers Monica's sweetness and patience encouraged them, along with her words of consolation. They knew that she suffered as much as they did in their loveless marriages.

Augustine writes that when her circle of friends asked her how she lived with such an excitable man and not be battered, Monica replied that there were two things necessary for domestic peace: firstly, she recalled the matrimonial contract which they agreed to; secondly she counseled silence when the husband was in a bad mood. By following her advice, Augustine added that many found peace and better treatment from their husbands.

Monica's neighbors benefited from her ability to minister in other ways as well. "Whenever she could," writes her son, "she used to act the part of peacemaker between souls in conflict over some quarrel, never tale-bearing except for such things as were likely to reconcile them. … She did her best to put an end to their quarrels by kind words. This was my mother's way, learned in the school of her heart, where Thou wast her secret teacher." Much to her joy, her faithfulness and patience with her husband eventually resulted into his coming to know Christ, as well as her contentious mother-in-law.

There were other children in the marriage beside the wayward Augustine. Augustine was the eldest, Navigius, was the middle child, and a daughter, Perpetua, completed the family. Monica had been unable to secure baptism for her children, and when Augustine fell ill her grief was overwhelming. In her great distress she begged her husband to allow him to be baptized. He agreed, but when the boy recovered, withdrew his consent. Their mother was deeply committed to raising her children to love Jesus Christ and St. Augustine writes: "From the time when my mother fed me at the breast, my infant heart had been suckled dutifully on His name, the name of the Son, my Saviour. Deep inside my heart His name remained and nothing could entirely captivate me, however learned, however nearly expressed, however true it might be, unless His name were in it."

For all the volatility of their father, he was a good father to Augustine and together with Monica made many sacrifices in order to educate their highly intellectual son. Navigius, the second son, appears occasionally in Augustine's writings, and their daughter, Perpetua, became the superior of a convent of nuns.

Augustine was indeed an extraordinary, intellectual man. He was a brilliant thinker and seemed to have a natural ability as a leader of men, if leading a group of rowdy, mischievous youth counted as such. Monica had thought that he would do well in a secular career and had strong, ambitious hopes that he would one day succeed. It even seems that she tried to arrange a socially advantageous marriage for him that turned out to be an utter disaster. Augustine not only states that he was wayward, but that he was also lazy. His father sent him away to school, to Madaura, and it was here that he fell into grievous sin. It does appear that Monica was literally wrestling with God for the very soul of her son.

Shortly after Augustine's journey to Carthage to pursue his studies, his father Patricius died and Monica resolved not to marry again. It was her great consolation that her husband had been received into the Church before his death, perhaps compensation for all she had to go through with Augustine. It was during his time in Carthage that the teachings of Manichean engulfed Augustine. When he returned home at the age of nineteen he sought to share his "enlightenment" with his mother. St. Monica was not only a mother who loved unconditionally, but was a mother who set boundaries with her troubled son. When he attempted to share the heretical and erroneous teachings, she unwaveringly refused to let him live under the same roof with her or eat at her table. He admits that despite her great love for him, "words cannot describe how dearly she loved me, [but] her love for catholic truth was greater.

In the *Confessions* Augustine dwells on his inner experiences rather that on the actual facts of his life. It was his mother's intense personal concern for his spiritual rebirth that occupies much of his writing. It is easy to understand his natural, loving preoccupation with his mother. For without the intercession of his persistent, faithful mother, he would never have responded to the Gospel message, which he finally did, accepting Christ in the year 386 on the eve of celebrating Resurrection Day.

St. Augustine's most eloquent writings pour forth the long years of his mother's incessant tears and prayers on his behalf:

> "Night and day my mother poured out her tears to Thee and offered her heart-blood in sacrifice for Thou didst rescue my soul from the depths of this darkness [Manicheeism] because my mother, Thy faithful servant, wept to Thee for me, shedding more tears for my spiritual death than other mothers shed for the bodily death of a son."

Any mother can understand her heartbreak. This beloved son, embarking on a life devoid of the saving grace of Christ. Her hope was buoyed when she had a dream that lifted her prayers to another level of intensity. "She dreamed," he writes, "that she was standing on a wooden rule, and coming toward her in a halo of splendor she saw a young man who smiled at her in joy, although she herself was sad and quite consumed with grief. He asked her the reason for her sorrow and her daily tears, not because he did not know, but because he had some thing to tell her, for this is what happens in visions. When she replied that her tears were for the son she had lost, he told her to take heart, for if she looked carefully, she would see that where she was, there also was I. And when she looked she saw me standing beside her on the same rule."

Though the vision in St. Monica's dream was indeed heavenly reassurance, she nonetheless continued in her quest for her son's salvation: "This chaste, devout, and prudent woman, a widow such as is close to Thy heart, never ceased to pray at all hours and offer Thee the tears she shed for me. The dream had given new spirit to her hope, but she gave no rest to her sighs and her tears."

Rejecting all that his family had suggested and hoped for him, Augustine looked scornfully on his mother's religion and instead undertook the study of a variety of pagan philosophies for clues to the meaning of life. Upon undertaking an opportunity to begin a career as an orator and teacher of the art of oratory [rhetoric], he moved from Africa to Rome and thence to Milan, at that time the seat of government in Italy. During this time his mother sought council from a holy bishop, whose name is not given, but who consoled her with the now famous words, "the child of those tears shall never perish."

It is no surprise to find that Monica followed her son, the object of her passionate prayers, to Milan a few years later, and would have traveled with him to Rome as well, if events had played out differently. She resolutely determined to see her son a Catholic before she died and thus she set across the sea pursuing her son and her goal for his conversion. To envision this dear mother crossing seas, traveling lonely roads, a stranger seeking solace in the knowledge that this one that was lost would now be found, well it is indeed heart breaking. Can anyone of us imagine going to the lengths that Monica went to bring her firstborn son into redemption? It is astounding, but it speaks volumes to the extent a parent will go for their child. It touches our hearts with the understanding that God reaches out to us in the same, devoted way. He loves us with His entire being.

To know that this beloved son was actually trying to outwit his mother and stay one step ahead of her in this somewhat tragic game of cat and mouse is hard to comprehend. Augustine was aware of his mother's desire to travel with him to Rome to be by his side. One can understand that at twenty-nine years of age, this son did not wish to be supervised or pressed in upon by his mother, but his deceit was shameful. Stubborn, strong-willed and obviously dishonest, Augustine told his mother that he needed to say goodbye to a friend before they left for Rome and she should return to the inn where they were staying. Upon returning to the inn her manipulative son sailed away from his mother. He may have been able to escape her physical presence, but he would never escape her persistent, intentional prayers. Upon realizing what he had done Monica wept, continuing, undaunted, to pray for his conversion.

As we now realize, Monica was not one to be easily deterred. Following her son at a discreet time later, she eventually found St. Ambrose. His inspired preaching and influence on her son gave her the ultimate joy of her life, the beautiful conversion of Augustine. After seventeen years of defiant resistance, he finally yielded and accepted Christ as his Lord and Savior at the age of thirty-three.

Monica was to find further joy when not only did Augustine decide to become a Christian, but vowed to live out his live in service to God. Of course this did not occur right away but eventually took root in his heart over time. Through the formation of a small group of friends gathered at Cassiacum in the fall of 386 with Monica as housemother, a type of community was formed. This held an immense attraction for Augustine and it was here that Monica manifested a new and surprising facet of her character.

In St. Augustine's book, *The Happy Life*, he records the dialogue that he is having between his friends about what makes for a happy life. When Monica happens into the room and hears their discussion, she adds her thoughts to the lively foray with this discourse: "If he wishes to possess good things, his is happy; if he desires evil things, no matter if he possesses them, his is wretched." It was this conversation that revealed the very depths of Monica's spirit and gave the group its real focus. Augustine commended her and told her she was a masterful philosopher and compared her to Cicero himself.

The delighted Monica and beloved son spent the next six months in peaceful companionship at Cassiacum, after which time Augustine was baptized in the church of St. John the Baptist at Milan. The call to return to Africa was great, so the two, mother and son, set out on their journey, stopping at Civita Vecchia, and then at Ostia, a main port near Rome.

This is where the greatest story of a mother's love for a son comes to an end. Augustine tells of the moving spiritual experience that he and his mother shared while waiting for passage to Africa. As they lingered by a window enjoying a lovely garden view, Monica expressed to her son the deep, profound peace that enveloped her and the conviction that her life's task had been completed. It was very shortly afterward that she fell seriously ill with a fever. She died two days later and was buried in the town in which she waited for safe passage home.

Although Augustine grieved the passing of his mother, friends told him that she would not feel sad to be buried in a foreign land. It was recounted to him that she had said, with a touch of humor that she was sure God would remember where she was buried and raise her up. She had previously told Augustine and his brother Navigius: "Lay this body anywhere, and take no trouble over me. One thing only do I ask of you, that you remember me at the altar of the Lord wherever you may be."

St. Monica's remains are venerated in the church of St. Augustine, Rome, Italy, removed from Ostia sometime in the sixth century. But you can be reassured that spiritually Monica resides in the presence of her Christ, Jesus, King of kings and Lord of lords. It was for Him that she lived and for her children, especially for the prodigal child, Augustine, for whom she would leave no stone unturned but to see him in Heaven, along with her for eternity. This sweet mother spent seventeen years crying, caring, praying and believing not only for the soul of her wayward child, but for her husband, mother-in-law and all of her neighbors.

God knew that her tears, disappointments, and prayers served to draw her closer to Him, thus drawing the lost to know Him as well. A model for domestic peace and stability, honor among women and the sacrificial love of a mother's heart, Monica, the mother of St. Augustine, was honored as a saint in her own right.

Scripture Application

SOON AFTERWARD, JESUS WENT TO
A TOWN, CALLED NAIN, AND HIS
DISCIPLES AND A LARGE CROWD WENT
ALONG WITH HIM. AS HE APPROACHED
THE TOWN GATE, A DEAD PERSON
WAS BEING CARRIED OUT—THE ONLY
SON OF HIS MOTHER AND SHE WAS A
WIDOW. AND A LARGE CROWD FROM
THE TOWN WAS WITH HER. WHEN THE
CROWD SAW HER, HIS HEART WENT
OUT TO HER AND HE SAID, "DON'T
CRY." THEN HE WENT AND TOUCHED
THE COFFIN, AND THOSE CARRYING IT
STOOD STILL. HE SAID, "YOUNG MAN I
SAY TO YOU, GET UP!" THE DEAD MAN
SAT UP AND BEGAN TO TALK AND JESUS
GAVE HIM BACK TO HIS MOTHER.

LUKE 7:11-15

Reflections on Faithful Intercessory Prayer

Have you ever been called to pray for the lost? A child or some other loved one? Perhaps even a neighbor or stranger?

Has anyone ever prayed for your salvation? Can you think of a time you knew others must be praying for you?

Have you ever been awakened at night with the thought that you needed to pray for someone who had just come to mind? What was the outcome?

SUNFLOWER

REACHING UP INTO THE HEAVENS THIS VIBRANT SUNFLOWER PROCLAIMS,
"HERE AM I, LORD! SEND ME!" ALIVE AND BEAUTIFUL, THE SUNFLOWER
ENCOURAGES ALL WHO WITNESS ITS GLORIOUS PRESENCE.
IRENA SENDLER IS LIKE THE SUNFLOWER—SHE WENT WHERE SHE WAS
NEEDED TO BRING LIGHT AND LIFE TO THE CHILDREN OF THE STORM.

Irena Sendler

1910 – 2008

Mother of the Children of the Holocaust

It is difficult to understand the type of faith one must possess in order to save someone's life. Not only the faith to save one, but to save 2,500 children from certain death. To repeatedly step into personal danger and risk everything so the innocent could live is an example of Christ's love for the world. So when a young woman readily accepted the task of rescuing babies and children from the Nazis' evil grip, we see true faith in action. This was an incredible act of selfless faith and devotion, a profound faith, a faith that never faltered or wavered for even a moment. Her heart resolved that every child would make it out of the Warsaw Ghetto alive, or she would die trying. She almost did.

Irena Krzyzanowski was born into the small town of Otwock, just fifteen miles southeast of Warsaw, Poland. Irena's father, Stanislaw, was a great influence on his young daughter's life during her formative, impressionable years at home. Stanislaw was a physician and one of the first Polish Socialists. Many of his patients were poor Jews. His ideas motivated Irena to want to help those less fortunate than she, and she hoped to make a difference in others' lives.

Irena's mind was eager as she read through and studied Polish literature, and her national pride led her to join the leftist Union of Democratic Youth. The Jewish people of Poland stirred her heart. Her compassion for them lay deep within her being, having been nurtured there by her caring father. It was also her deep faith in God, instilled in her by the Catholic Church, that lay the foundation for her future heroic deeds. Irena's love of Jesus Christ and His truths gave her the strength to undertake an unbelievable feat in history's darkest days.

It only seemed natural that Irena would become a social worker as an adult, and she worked as a senior administrator in the Warsaw Social Welfare Department. Through this department she helped run the canteens of the city during the invasion of the German troops in 1939. These canteens not only provided food, but offered financial aid, clothing, medicine, and other much needed services for poor Jewish families. In a wise move they registered their Jewish patients under fictitious names and often listed them as suffering from highly contagious diseases.

In 1940, the Nazis built the now infamous Warsaw Ghetto to contain Poland's Jewish population where nearly 5,000 people died each month from starvation and an array of diseases. This ghetto was roughly the size of Central Park and become the home to 500,000 Jews, making it the largest Jewish community in the world outside New York. This "city" was surrounded by more than 10 miles (16km) of brick walls, up to 10 feet (3m) high and topped with broken glass, just to isolate the hated Juden [Jewish] population.

The conditions were appalling with seven people living in one room, struggling to survive with strict food rationing that eventually led to mass starvation. It was not uncommon to see beggars in the streets and sick children walking about in their bare feet in the cold of winter. Deadly typhus and tuberculosis epidemics broke out, adding even more horror to the already tortured families.

The Warsaw Ghetto was a fifty-block area that most non-Jewish Poles turned their backs on, but Irena could not bear to stand by and do nothing while thousands were being slaughtered. It was as if God devised this plan of Irena's position in the Welfare Department to enable her to gain access into the Ghetto. Disguised as a nurse and armed with an epidemic control pass, she was able to move freely within the confines of the Ghetto. She used this pass to visit daily with the sole aim of re-establishing contacts and providing food, medicines and much needed clothing. With her heart beating in solidarity and unity for the Jews, Irena wore a star armband at all times, the star that all Jews were ordered to wear for identification purposes, easily spotted by the Nazi guards.

It was during these visits to the Ghetto that Irena began to realize that unless she could convince the parents to let her smuggle their beautiful children out they would surely perish. The parents begged for assurance that their sons and daughters would survive being smuggled out with the added promise that someday they would be reunited. These two promises were not something Irena could give; there were too many variables in this risky equation, too many uncertainties involved. It was her unwavering promise of their children's impending death that finally settled the parents struggle in releasing their most prized possessions—their little ones. For the rest of Irena's life, the haunting cries of both parents and children as they were separated plagued her night and day.

Horrified, she resolved to help devise a plan where she and others could smuggle children out of the inhumanity of the Ghetto, thus giving them a chance to live. Because of her courage, faith, and sense of purpose, 2,500 Jewish children were saved from certain death.

To be able to successfully smuggle the children out of the Ghetto, Irena had to recruit outside help. The true blessing came as one person from the ten centers of the Social Welfare Department stepped forward to help initiate the plan Irena had devised. Armed with thousands of falsified documents with forged signatures, the children were given new identities and placed in Catholic orphanages, convents and Christian families.

The courthouse in the Ghetto became a very useful tool in smuggling the children out to safety. Ideally, it had two entrances, with one opening into the Ghetto and the other opening into the Aryan side of Warsaw. Escape was difficult, but with the help of those with the courage to assist, these refugees of the heart were placed in what was called Pogotowi Opiekuncze, or caring units. It was at the caring units that the children were given their false identities and then moved into the various places that had immediate openings for their safe haven.

Irena alone knew their true identities and actually kept records of their falsified names and their Jewish names, burying this information written on tissue paper and placed in glass jars that she buried beneath an apple tree. This tree just happened to be across the street from a German barracks, so the jars were buried right in the Nazis' own neighborhood. It was this enduring hope that Irena clung so fervently to, the hope that someday she could dig the jars up and locate all of the children and share with them about the sacrifices their parents made so they could live. A hope that kept her motivated, even though she was facing persecution in her own life.

Irena was able to smuggle out over 400 children between 1942 and 1943, but on October 20, she was arrested for her suspected activities and imprisoned by the Gestapo. It was here that she faced unmentionable torment from her captors, who insisted that she divulge all information about her children. It was this information, even in the face of death that she refused to give. Under the unrelenting torture of the Nazis who sought to break her, Irena held silent and resilient. During the brutal interrogation the guards broke both her feet and legs and in spite of her suffering she resolved to protect the children no matter the consequences. The ruthless, cold, unfeeling Gestapo sought to break her body, but they could not break her spirit. Though her body was savagely beaten, her mind battered by interrogation, she fought the good fight all for her precious little ones. The Nazis held her in the Pawiak prison for three months, and because she refused to betray her associates or surrender the locations where the children were hiding, they sentenced her to death.

Irena knew that her life lay in the hands of Almighty God, but her prayers were only for the continued safety of the children. As she awaited her fate, her Zegota associates were able to bribe one of the German guards with a backpack full of money to halt her impending execution. The Polish speaking German soldier led the unsuspecting Irena to a waiting car driving her out to the countryside where he knocked her unconscious. Dragging her limp and battered body out of the car, he left her alone and bleeding beside the road. After the soldier had driven away, Irena's Zegota associates descended on her, bearing her away to a "safe house," where they tended to her wounds with both medicine and compassion.

The German authorities, unaware that Irena had not been executed, posted the names of those who had been shot throughout the city, and she was listed among the dead. Irena read them herself, realizing just how close she had come to death.

"It is beyond description to tell you what you feel when traveling to your own execution and, at the last moment, you find you have been bought out," she said.

Irena went into hiding for a short time, but under a false identity she soon resumed rescuing the children from the horrors of the Warsaw Ghetto. A few weeks later her mother died, and SS officers turned up at her mother's funeral insisting that those attending tell where she was hiding. Her commitment to the little ones was so strong that not even her imprisonment, torture, and narrow escape from the Nazis could keep her from the children. She continued to smuggle them out until the end of the war.

In January 1945, the Red Army liberated Warsaw from the German army, and Irena dug up the glass jars she had buried. With hope in her heart she turned the lists with the detailed information over to the Jewish Committee, information that she prayed would help track down the 2,500 children she had help place in adoptive families.

It had always been her plan to reunite them with relatives scattered across Europe, but her heart sank when she realized that most of them had lost their families to the Nazi concentration camps.

Irena thought back to all of the children and how difficult it had been to smuggle them out of the Ghetto. Some were carried out in body bags, coffins, garbage cans, potato sacks, in ambulances as "victims" of typhus, and one tiny baby had even been taken out in a toolbox. Now, after all her planning and all the meticulous information she had painstakingly hidden in the hopes of a reuniting the children and their parents, it was all for naught. Nevertheless, she had saved the children. Yes, it was all for the children, but still she felt the anguish of the parents and grandparents they had lost, never to be seen again.

Irena's children only knew her by the code name Jolanta, and never imagined seeing their rescuer again in their lifetime. It wasn't until many years later when she had received an award for her humanitarian service during the war that many of the now grown children remembered her from the picture they saw in the newspaper. They had not forgotten the woman who had risked her life to save them from certain death. Irena received many telephone calls from "her children," who wanted to personally thank her from rescuing them from the Ghetto. They wanted her to know that they would never forget what she had so sacrificially, unselfishly did for them so long ago.

In her later years, Irena continued her work with Social Welfare, helping others by working to provide emergency services for children, to build orphanages, and create housing for the elderly. Irena had a daughter and son to raise and love as well, but I like to think of the 2,500 children she rescued as her children in spirit. In her very being, she was still prompted by her heart for people and her desire to provide hope and a better life for those less fortunate. It was her incredible faith in God and her love for Christ that encouraged her to tackle the unbelievable rescue mission that she so successfully completed.

Irena Sendler had lived her life as a humble servant, inspired by her father Stanislaw and moved by the times in which she lived. For Irena it was only natural that she should respond the way she did to the situation of the Warsaw Ghetto. She saw a desperate need and did something about it and would never consider not responding to the great suffering that she witnessed during World War II. Many others, she is quick to point out, came forward to help as well, and at one point she had as many as twenty-five people helping in the efforts to save the children. But it was Irena's perseverance and faith that led to the successful rescue of 2,500 children. Still she says, "I could have done more. This regret will follow me to my death." The thought of even one child left at the hands of the murderous Nazis broke her heart.

Irena Sendler is a hero to the world at large and especially to those who were the children rescued from certain death. Such character and love of her fellow man is incredibly inspiring. Irena Sendler is a true mother of faith.

The Story Behind the Story:
How Irena Sendler Was Discovered

In the fall of 1999 Mr. Norman Conard from Uniontown High School in Kansas encouraged three of his students to work on a year long project for National History Day that would, among other things, extend the boundaries of their classroom to families in the community, contribute to learning history, and teach others not only respect but tolerance. It would also fulfill their classroom motto: "He who changes one person, changes the world entire."

Three ninth grade girls, Megan Stewart, Elizabeth Cambers, and Sabrina Coons, accepted the challenge and decided to enter their project in the National History Day program. Mr. Conard showed them an article from a *U.S. News and World Report* published in March of 1994; it was entitled "Other Schindlers." He told the girls the article might be a typographical error since he had not heard of this woman or her story. The students began their research for primary and looked at secondary sources throughout the year. Another girl, Jessica Shelton, became interested in the project and joined the others as the research intensified.

Upon finding the truth concerning Irena's heroism the girls decided to write a play entitled *Life in a Jar*, in which they portrayed Irena's life. They have performed this for numerous clubs, religious organizations, and audiences throughout the state of Kansas, the U.S., and even Europe. As of October 2006, they had performed 170 presentations. The community of Uniontown has little diversity and no Jewish students in the school district, but became so inspired by the project that they decided to hold an Irena Sendler Day.

The students began to search for the final resting place of Irena and discovered she was still alive and living in Warsaw, Poland. Because Irena was living in rather bleak and impoverished conditions, they resolved that at each performance of *Life in a Jar* they would put out a glass jar and collect funds for Irena and other Polish rescuers. The significance of this project really started to grow with numerous contacts. These contacts assisted the girls in sending the funds to Poland for the care of Irena and the other rescuers.

The girls wrote letters to Irena, and she wrote deeply meaningful letters to them with such comments as, "You're continuing the effort I started over fifty years ago; you are my dearly beloved girls." Irena's own words summed up her feelings about the Kansas girls' efforts on her behalf. "I am stunned and fascinated; very, very surprised; interested."

The girls experienced great emotional situations in life, as had later members of the project. Megan, whose role was that of Irena in the presentation, lost her mother, who was only forty, to cancer in the summer of 2006.

The students dreamed of visiting Warsaw to interview Irena, the surviving children that she rescued, and others connected to the story. In January of 2001, they performed before a large school district in a city about one hundred miles from their school. A Jewish educator and businessman saw the performance and invited Mr. Conard and his students to have lunch with him that day. The great news was that he was interested in raising the funds to send the girls to Warsaw that spring to bring back Irena's story. This kind businessman was able to raise all the money needed in twenty-four hours.

So it was that in May of 2001, Mr. Conard traveled with four students, several parents, and others, to Warsaw, Poland. There they spent precious time with Irena, hearing in person all the stories of her amazing rescue efforts to save Jewish children from sure death. The most exciting part of their pilgrimage was when the Polish organization for the Children of the Holocaust arranged a meeting with the rescuers and the children that were saved. The girls met a famous Polish poet who was saved by Irena and an author of a well-known memoir of the Holocaust, who called the students "rescuers of the rescuer." The Polish press made this story international news, and now Irena's story was finally reaching others. The group met Elzibieta Ficowska and heard her beautiful story of being rescued by Irena at the age of five months, carried out in a carpenter's box.

The story of Irena Sendler is covering the globe through magazine articles, TV stations and newspapers. Upon finding this website on Irena and The Project, I could not even fathom not sharing Irena and the students' heroic story on these pages. There is a book being written about Irena, and at this time a movie is being planned with Angelina Jolie to star as Irena.

Many people are involved in releasing her story of courage and faith. Her family, many of the children she rescued, and the students involved in the Irena Sendler Project are committed to sharing Irena with the world. Perhaps you would like to help as well. I encourage you to visit The Irena Sendler Project and see how you can bring the *Life in a Jar* presentation to your church, school, or community. Remember what Mr. Conard's class motto says: "He who changes one person, changes the world entire."

To see how you can help rescue the rescuers, please visit **www.irenasendler.org.**

POSTSCRIPT

Irena Sendler passed away May 12, 2008, at 8 A.M. in Warsaw, Poland. She passed away peacefully, knowing that her message goes on. Our hearts and prayers go out to her worldwide family. She is gone, but will never be forgotten. She was recently nominated for the Nobel Peace Prize. Her legacy of repairing the world continues as good continues to triumph over evil. Irena Sendlerowa was 98 years old.

The www.irenasendler.org web site tells more about Irena's life (under home page and additional information). The *Life in a Jar* students who brought her story to worldwide attention, continue to share her legacy and the play with people all over the world.

Scripture Application

DEFEND THE CAUSE OF THE
WEAK AND FATHERLESS;
MAINTAIN THE RIGHTS OF
THE POOR AND OPPRESSED,
RESCUE THE WEAK AND NEEDY;
DELIVER THEM FROM THE
HAND OF THE WICKED.

PSALM 82:3-4

Reflections on Faithful Courage:

When Irena faced the dangers of rescuing the children from the Warsaw Ghetto do you think she counted the cost?

What would you do if a situation presented itself and you could make a difference?

Could you face your giants through your faith in Christ? Would you be willing to lay down your life to save someone else?

QUEEN ANNE'S LACE

DELICATE, REGAL, AND MOST OF ALL LADYLIKE IN ALL ITS DISPLAY IN
THE GARDEN, QUEEN ANNE'S LACE CAPTURES THE ESSENCE OF LADY
MARGARET BEAUFORT. THIS ELEGANT BUT HUMBLE FLOWER CAN BE
FOUND ON LONELY ROADSIDES AND ROCKY HILLS. LADY MARGARET WAS
OFTEN FOUND HELPING THE DESTITUTE AND THOSE IN NEED.

Margaret Beaufort

1443 – 1509

Mother of King Henry the VII

Lady Margaret Beaufort was a grand woman of faith and humility, generous of heart as well as generous with her wealth and time. As the mother of the future king of England, Henry the VII, one would imagine that her life was one of comfort and ease. But this was not the case for the privileged young woman who was born the only child and heiress to John Beaufort, the first Duke of Somerset, grandson to John of Gaunt, Duke of Lancaster, and great grandson of Edward III.

Margaret was only three years old when her father died leaving her in the sole care of her devoted mother, Margaret Beauchamp. Margaret was married while still very young, to Edmund Tudor, Earl of Richmond, by whom she had a son, Henry, their only child.

History was repeated when Edmund died leaving his wife a young widow with their fifteen-week-old son to care for alone. Margaret chose a new husband in a cousin on both her mother's side and father's side of her family, Lord Henry Stafford, who could trace his roots to Henry III.

Margaret and Lord Henry were married in 1459 and their union lasted twenty-three years but produced no children for the couple. Margaret's third husband was the Earl of Derby who died in 1504.

These are just the bare facts and statistics of Margaret Beaufort's life. The real story about Margaret is found in the accounts that tell how she lived her life and just how her faith touched and ministered to others.

Lady Beaufort was a pious and devout woman who was known far and wide for her charitable works with the poor and destitute. Rising every morning at five o'clock, she spent the next few hours in prayer and devotions ending at around ten o'clock when she began to tend to the poor. Even though she was the mother of the King, she was often found dressing the wounds of bedraggled beggars, treating them with her medicinal skills and relieving their distress.

Margaret's heart was full of compassion for those who were without the wherewithal to make ends meet, and she often kept up to twelve people in her house where she fed and clothed them. With her acts of benevolence, devotion to prayer and meditation, Margaret gave her life as she believed her Savior did, loving God and serving mankind.

Historians might raise their eyebrows at her seemingly aesthetic way of life, but Margaret had a distinct calling to follow Christ with her whole being. Not only did she give of her time, money and heart to the poor and religious houses, she also gave money to academia. Lady Margaret Beaufort was a generous patroness of learning and through her contributions she established readerships in divinity at Oxford and Cambridge. As a patroness to the universities she instituted two public lectures of divinity at both colleges only to be surpassed by her provision to God's House at Cambridge, which was re-established as Christ's College due to her significant funding. She provided the funding for the founding of St. John's College as well. Not only was Lady Margaret Beaufort the mother of the King of England, she was a mother of students at both universities and patroness of all the learned men of England.

There may be some critical asides concerning Margaret's life, but most historians agree that these came about because of the age in which she lived. Because of her compassion for the poor and her dedication to the pillars of academia, historians applaud Margaret's acts of civil duty while Christians uphold her for her faith and virtue.

Patroness of universities, benevolent contributor to the poor and mother of King Henry VII, Lady Margaret was many things to many people. But there is one thing for certain. Margaret Beaufort was indeed first and foremost a devout woman of faith.

Scripture Application

RELIGION THAT GOD OUR
FATHER ACCEPTS AS PURE AND
FAULTLESS IS THIS: TO LOOK
AFTER ORPHANS AND WIDOWS
IN THEIR DISTRESS AND
KEEP ONESELF FROM BEING
POLLUTED BY THE WORLD.

JAMES 1:27

Reflections on Compassion

Do you have a heart for the poor and dispossessed? Do you make it a priority to give to those less fortunate than yourself?

Have you ever been in need before and benefitted from the charitable actions of others? What was it like to be on the receiving end of compassion?

Is there a cause or organization that you are passionate about? Outside the Church, there are organizations or institutions that count on your giving in order to serve the community. What one cause could you become enthused about in life?

ENGLISH LAVENDER PROVIDES A COVERING FOR THE GARDEN—A LANDSCAPE FOR OTHER BLOOMS TO JOIN. THE VIBRANCY OF PURPLE LIFTS THE SPIRITS AND THE FRAGRANCE SOOTHES THE SOUL. HOW BLESSED SUSANNAH WESLEY'S FAMILY WAS IN HAVING HER STRENGTH OF PRESENCE WITH THEM TO GUIDE AND CHALLENGE THEM IN THEIR FAITH.

Susannah Wesley

1669 – 1742

Mother of John Wesley

Most of us hope and pray that we might leave a legacy of some sort to encourage and inspire others to know God. It is with this fervent prayer that we recognize a woman from an era when women were not often allowed to share the Gospel of Jesus Christ.

Susannah Wesley was a wife, mother and dedicated servant in the kingdom of God. True, she was first and foremost a wife and mother of ten surviving children from a total of nineteen births, but it was the role of mother that fulfilled her lasting legacy.

Susannah was very well versed in how a clergyman's home should run, especially one that was spilling over with a large brood. Born on January 20, 1669, to London pastor Samuel

Annesley, she was the youngest of twenty-five children. Large families were a natural for Susannah, so when she married Samuel Wesley, a newly ordained Anglican Minister, it was just a fact of life that she would have a boisterous clan of her own. Samuel Wesley had been born into a family of extreme poverty, his father a dissenting pastor of the Church of England's 1662 Act of Conformity that required all ministers to abide by the Book of Common Prayer. Because Samuel's father refused to be cowed into subjection by the Church's assertive demands, he was forced out of his parish and his home. Like most of the other 2,000 so-called "Non-Conformist" pastors during this time, Pastor Wesley had to subsist on teaching, preaching or writing wherever he could.

Samuel, born in 1662 at the crux of the Church of England's push for supremacy, grew up within his family's struggle for survival. However when it came time for him to decide which church he would align himself with as a pastor, he chose the Church of England, which allowed him to attend Oxford University. Unfortunately his living conditions as a student there were not much better than he had experienced at home. Samuel was forced to live on an extremely strict budget that left little room for any luxuries.

It was during his time of study at Oxford that Samuel was first introduced to Susannah. Many of the university students enjoyed spending time at Reverend Annesley's home and engaging him in lively, intellectual conversation. It was during one of these informal visits that Samuel met Susannah and was quite taken with her charm and inquisitive exuberance. The stimulating ideas and information were an ideal way for Susannah to add to her education as well as developing a friendship with Samuel Wesley.

Susannah and Samuel Wesley were married in 1689 soon after he was ordained when she was twenty and he was twenty-eight. Susannah embraced the Anglican Church as well and together they began a life of religious devotion when the whole of England was in the midst of an all-time low of national spiritual apathy. A decline in faith resulted in most seeing God as a very disinterested, withdrawn Creator who cared little for the day-to-day drudgery of his creation. This lack of knowledge of Almighty God resulted in Deism and church services had become dull, dry and filled with cold, dreary logic. It was during this drab, spiritual void that Samuel Wesley began his ministry, serving in a variety of parishes until he finally settled in Epworth in the north Lincolnshire area in 1696, where he would serve for most of his life. Susannah had produced seven children in their seven years traveling about serving other parishes, but she lost three of them.

This would prove to be the case for Susannah's child-bearing years—babies born and babies dying—yet ten of Susannah's eventual nineteen children lived to maturity. It seemed that she spent a great deal of time "churching"—the Prayer Book's "Service of Thanksgiving following Childbirth"—making it an annual occasion. This made for a large family to care for in all aspects of child-rearing—educating, assigning chores and raising them to be decent, upright children, who one scholar described as "a cluster of bright, vehement boys and girls, living by a clean and high code, and on the plainest fare; but drilled to soft tones, to pretty formal courtesies, with learning as an ideal, duty as an atmosphere, and fear of God as law."

On top of all this Susannah carried out all her household duties, often with only one servant to help in corralling all the children and insurmountable work that had to be attended to regularly. On top of the children and chores, Susannah took on the responsibility of the business expenses of the church, as

Samuel had no business acumen at all. She did this all without complaint or criticism of her husband's lack of business sense. Not to say that there were never differences between them. Even though they were entirely devoted to each other, there were occasions when they would disagree, each having very strong characters and definite opinions on a variety of subjects.

Both Susannah and Samuel were passionate about their political views, which at times could prove unsettling in their marriage. Samuel stood squarely behind King William, the Dutch son-in-law of the king whom he had overthrown in 1688. Susannah was a staunch supporter of King James and when Samuel offered a prayer for King William during family prayers Susannah refused to say "Amen." This not only caused disagreement, it also instituted a separation for a time. Samuel remarking to his wife as he left home, "Sukey, we must part for if we have two kings we must have two beds." Susannah was hesitant to offer an apology and asserted that she would apologize if she was wrong, but she felt to do so for expediency would be a lie and thus a sin. Eventually husband and wife were able to reunite five months later when King William died. From their reconciliation John Wesley was born in 1703. John described this event later as his mother being "inflexible," and his father equally so.

Life was not ideal and often was very difficult for the family when parishioners protested against Samuel's political choices. In 1705 a group of villagers harassed Susannah and her children while Samuel was away from home. All night they shouted, fired guns and drummed loudly outside the parsonage. This raucous, persistent noise continued through the night as poor Susannah tried to recover from just delivering her sixteenth child. The new baby had a nurse, but because of the stress and exhaustion from the ongoing disturbance she slipped into a deep sleep, rolled over on the babe and smothered it.

There were times that the locals would be so opposed to Samuel as pastor that they would mock the children, burn the family crops, damage the rectory and even abuse the family cows and dog. When a parishioner demanded immediate payment of a debt that Samuel could not pay, he actually had him arrested. This from his own parishioner no less, who gave no thought at all to the pastor's wife and children who struggled to survive on a meager budget. Samuel meanwhile became self-appointed pastor to his fellow inmates making the most of a dreary and despondent situation. Finally the church paid off the debt and Samuel was able to return home to Susannah and his brood.

Tragedy struck yet again on February 9, 1709 when the family battled a blaze in the Epworth Rectory. This fire not only affected the family as a whole, but put John in a particularly dangerous situation. Susannah, pregnant with what would be her last child, scrambled with her family to safety, but upon assembling the rescued, she realized she was missing one of the children. Six year old John was standing high up in a window with red and yellow flames dancing about him. A neighbor lifted another man to his shoulders so the second man could snatch the little boy to safety just seconds before the roof collapsed, engulfing the whole of it in an inferno. John felt that God had saved him and delivered him, referring to himself as a literal "brand snatched from the burning."

Because there was so many of them, the family had to be separated and sent to live among a variety of relatives while the rectory was being rebuilt. Surviving the terror of the fire they thanked God for their safety, but realized that they had lost all the contents of their home including the family's papers and Samuel's library. John later considered the fire to have been set by a vindictive neighbor, although he conceded that it could have been accidental. Either way he almost perished in the intense flames that destroyed the rectory.

Susannah was able to manage her large household and properly educate her children by establishing a definite routine designed to produce maturity and develop Christian character. Susannah's policy was "strength guided by kindness," and she followed it through with each of her children during a time when strict discipline and severe punishment was a standard part of education. Susannah also determined to spend individual time with each of her children, purposely giving special attention to each and every one of them. John later wrote to his mother fondly remembering their special time alone.

Because of Susannah and Samuel's strong personalities there continued to be occasional conflicts in their family life. In 1711 Samuel was attending a long church conference and left his pulpit in charge of another minister, a Mr. Inman. This man proved to be a very poor choice since most of his sermon's centered on repaying one's debts, and Samuel was known to owe many. Some of the parishioners saw this as a slap in Samuel's face, and he was not even around to protest or defend himself.

It was during this time that Susannahh began a Sunday evening family gathering where they sang psalms, prayed, and Susannah read a short sermon from her husband's library.

She saw little harm in this since there was no official service on Sunday evening, but what began as just the family, soon became the servants and neighbors who had heard what was taking place at the Wesley home. Soon there were too many for the parsonage and Mr. Inman feared the competition and wrote a letter to Samuel complaining to him about what his wife was doing. Susannah had written Samuel about the gathering and thought there was no harm in coming together to worship while he was away. Mr. Inman claimed that such irregular services could cause criticism or even scandal for the church. The very idea of a woman having any part in a worship service, even in her own home was, well, unheard of at that time in history. Because of Mr. Inman's persistent letter, Samuel suggested to Susannah that she have someone else read the sermons. But the complaints still came from the unsettled Mr. Inman and finally Samuel told Susannah to discontinue the meetings. Susannah declined her husband's request to stop the meetings, explaining that the gatherings were a legitimate time of worship and a very effective ministry. Besides, Mr. Inman was the only one who seemed to object to the meetings, so she saw no real reason to stop. The services continued.

In spite of failing health, Samuel pursued his life long ambition to continue writing on his project, a book called *Dissertations on the Book of Job*. It had always been his hope that the book would succeed in publication and the financial gain would provide his family with all they would need for the remainder of their lives. This would not prove to be the case. This ponderous, scholarly tome was written in Latin and it did not appeal to the average reader. There would have been much more success if Samuel had only given himself to writing shorter, more popular pieces. It was his desire to give his talents and gifts to writing that he considered high scholarship.

Samuel Wesley would never overcome his lifelong struggle to remain out of debt, and on his death on April 5, 1735, John finally paid off all his debts. Susannah had very little and for the rest of her life she had to depend on her children for everything.

John Wesley and his brother Charles joined a group of colonists settling in Georgia, searching for spiritual fulfillment. It was through their journeys to America and back to England that they finally found the peace and assurance they sought. Their conversion not only fulfilled them spiritually, but also inspired them to begin the definitive preaching and outreach that would be a part of their new ministry. This style of preaching was dubbed Methodism after a "methodical" religious routine John had developed while at Oxford.

Susannah was moved into the center of this new ministry in London in a former cannon factory known as the Foundery. The large building held a school, a clinic, chapels, and living quarters for John and other workers. Susannah spent the rest of her life with her children nearby and among loving people who were involved in the new ministry. When Susannah faced the end of her life and with her children surrounding her she instructed them: "Children, as soon as I am released sing a psalm of praise to God." She then passed from this life to forever with her Lord and Savior, Jesus Christ, on July 23, 1742.

This dear mother's legacy stands firmly routed in her determination to raise her children with love and consistency, based on the teachings of the Bible. Her love for God and her Savior gave her the purpose and wherewithal to pursue the good life of service to others. Influence and example were her gift to her children, especially John, who gave of himself so the world would hunger for the righteousness of God. John Wesley was a dedicated servant of God who impacted the world for Jesus Christ, and it was due in large part to his mother's influence in the Epworth parsonage where her heart and hand guided him.

John Wesley was said by one scholar to have been the man who "represents the force which has most profoundly affected English history," referring to the 18th century.

Susannah Wesley expressed a simple desire in her lifetime: "I am content to fill a little space if God be glorified."

Scripture Application

I CAN DO EVERYTHING
THROUGH HIM WHO GIVES
ME STRENGTH.

PHILIPPIANS 4:13

Reflections on Faith for Needed Strength

When faced with difficulties have you been able to remain focused on your faith instead of circumstances? If not, how can you resist worry and frustration in the midst of turmoil?

As followers of Christ how can we retain focus and strength when struggling with life's unplanned events?

When you feel your weakest do you run to people or the Lord for help? Why?

TRUMPET FLOWER
HERALDING ALL IN THE GARDEN, THE TRUMPET FLOWER'S BOLD PETALS
CALL ATTENTION TO THE AWE-INSPIRING CREATOR. THE ONE WHO LOVES
ALL OF CREATION DIED FOR YOU, JESUS CHRIST, OUR SAVIOR. CATHERINE
BOOTH DETERMINED NOT TO LEAVE THIS EARTH WITHOUT ANNOUNCING
THIS MESSAGE TO THE LOST AND IMPOVERISHED OF THE WORLD.

Catherine Booth

1829 – 1890

Mother of The Salvation Army

There are many great ministries that grace the world with their presence, demonstrating the love of Christ to the suffering and lost. But The Salvation Army stands above the rest in its longevity and service to mankind. Through natural disasters such as Hurricanes Katrina and Rita, through the terrorist bombings of the Twin Towers, to the every day ministry to the down and out, The Salvation Army has been available for more than a century.

Catherine Booth and her husband William founded the now well-known Salvation Army in London, England, when local churches refused to care for the poor. It was this willingness to step in where others faltered that has propelled the Army into the epitome of world ministry that we all trust and respect. Catherine Booth's life reflects her own words: "We are made for larger ends than Earth can encompass. Oh, let us be true to our exalted destiny."

Catherine Mumford was born on January 17, 1829, and raised in Nottingham, England, to parents who were both strict in their political beliefs and religious practices. Catherine's concerned mother kept her daughter at home to complete her education due to ill health. It was during this time of solitude that Catherine began to study God's Holy Word, reading and devouring the Bible several times a day during her childhood. Her father met his match in debating with his teenage daughter who loved to delve in and debate social issues over dinner.

Thought to be quite the intellectual, Catherine was one day encouraged to critique a young, traveling minister who was passing through town. William Booth's charm was very evident to his admiring critic and the congregation's attention was held rapt through his passionate message. Because William's charm and intellect were hard to bypass, he and Catherine became instant friends and betrothed before he was assigned to some distant new post far from London. Through their three-year separation the young couple exchanged many letters with Catherine posting many warnings. She expressed her concern for his thinking on the position and views on women in ministry and the fleeting emotional experience of the power of the pulpit. She no doubt wanted him to see the validity of staying in one place to minister, providing a stable environment for a wife and family. It was also her desire for her future husband to recognize the calling of women to the ministry of God.

They were married in 1855 with William still traveling the English countryside and the dutiful Catherine staying at home to raise their growing family. Her fragile health was still of great concern. Of her eight children one daughter was born with severe disabilities so it was highly unlikely that she would ever be able to join her husband. It was within this physical limitation that Catherine began her writing career. Delivering a rebuttal to a local minister who demeaned women's spiritual understanding, she singlehandedly set out to change the status of women in the church. She self-published books and took speaking engagements, funneling any monies back into her husband's growing ministry to the poor.

Finally William left his position as a travelling preacher and set up The Christian Mission in London in 1865. This operation began with a group of recently converted volunteers and soon became a well-oiled organization that ministered to the downtrodden, forgotten poor in London's notorious East End. With practical assistance, providing food, warm clothing and medical help, The Christian Mission provided the lost with the Good News of Jesus Christ. It was Catherine who first recognized the potential for the greater possibilities of their work, evangelizing the world. This would be an army—an army set on nothing less than the salvation of the world.

This was easier said than done, as volunteer workers were harassed on the streets, sometimes being physically assaulted as they marched through the streets with their signs and musical instruments calling everyone to their outdoor tent meetings. When William returned home at night he was often soaked in liquor, mud and rotten eggs that had been thrown at him during his crusades in the mean streets of the East End. Even health concerns could not keep Catherine from participating in strategic meetings concerning the ministry. At her bedside in 1878 one such meeting took place and the name of the Mission was officially changed to The Salvation Army.

It was William and Catherine's personal dedication and commitment to all areas of the Army that caused the booming ministry to flourish. With enthusiastic volunteers formed from recent converts the Army moved with spirit and energy from their personal testimonies to family and friends. It was through tent meetings and the willingness of the volunteers to give of their time and money that the Army was propelled into a first rate organization in reaching out to the destitute. With Catherine's help William was able to maintain guidelines for each rank in the Army, and fashioned official army uniforms when public appearances became more formal than saloons and brothels.

All of the eight Booth children became involved in their parents' work and at least two of them were the Army's first missionaries to other continents. The sons-in-law of William Booth often took the family name as part of their own surname in order to formally align themselves with the now respected family. In his biography of mother-in-law Catherine, Franklin Booth-Tucker explained how the couple's ministry began in the home and kept expanding until it reached the whole world.

Having raised eight children, with little formal education, this frail, sickly woman managed to inspire thousands to rally together in an Army that would bring salvation to a desperate, hope-deprived world. On October 4, 1890, Catherine Mumford Booth died of breast cancer. At her funeral some 36,000 friends and converts were in attendance to pay honor to the woman they considered the mother of the Salvation Army.

William spent the remainder of his life continuing to minister to the working poor in London, visiting foreign Army stations, and writing manuals for future soldiers to live and work by. When he finally succumbed to death in 1912, the Salvation Army had 9,315 units throughout the world. Every Christmas Catherine's bells ring faithfully in ninety-four countries around the world, compelling its inhabitants to give in the hopes of easing another's suffering. This grand Army of noble men and women came about as the result of one woman's desire to make a difference in the lives of the poor and the lost.

Thus it is with fondness and a charitable hope that we remember Catherine Mumford Booth, "The Mother of the Salvation Army."

Scripture Application

"FOR I WAS HUNGRY AND YOU GAVE ME SOMETHING TO EAT, I WAS THIRSTY AND YOU GAVE ME SOMETHING TO DRINK, I WAS A STRANGER AND YOU INVITED ME IN. I NEEDED CLOTHES AND YOU CLOTHED ME, I WAS SICK AND YOU LOOKED AFTER ME, I WAS IN PRISON AND YOU CAME TO VISIT ME."

MATTHEW 25:35

Reflections on the Faith of Compassion

Have you ever realized that there was a need in your community or church and stepped up to fill the need? If not, how can you find a situation that needs help and resolve the problem?

Think about your passion and talent and see where your particular gifts might fit in and make a difference.

It is through God's compassionate love that we can have mercy for the suffering and afflicted among us.

Faith

of

Martyrs and Saints

Introduction to
Part Two

Faith of Martyrs and Saints

Those of us who are members of the Body of Christ, God's Church, understand that we are called "saints," meaning "true believers," and that we all bear witness to the standing we have because of Christ's sacrifice for us. The promise of Jesus' gift of eternal life lies in our hearts and minds, and because of what He did while we were still sinners we will have no part of the second death. We, the saints, carry the promise of eternal life in our very being and our lives may be asked of us because of our beliefs. The saints and the martyrs cry out to us telling of the request made of them while they lived in the world.

In Revelation 6:10 we read their cries in this passage: "They called out in a loud voice, 'How long Sovereign Lord, holy and true, until you judge the inhabitants of the earth and avenge our blood?' Then each of them was given a white robe, and they were told to wait a little longer, until the number of their fellow servants and brothers who were to be killed as they had been was completed."

We know that many have been martyred for standing faithful to Christ in all manners of circumstances. From the first recorded martyr, Stephen, in the book of Acts, to the modern day persecution of converts in nations throughout the worlds, martyred saints are crying out to God for justice. All manner of sufferings and torture have been pressed upon the believers who took their stand among the heroes of the faith. From beheadings, crucifixions, drownings and being burned at the stake, martyrs have given their very lives for Christ.

Revelation 19:8 proclaims the testimony of the saints in this manner:

> Then I heard what sounded like a great multitude, like the roar of rushing waters and like loud peals of thunder shouting:
> "Hallelujah! For our Lord God Almighty reigns.
> Let us rejoice and be glad and give him glory.
> For the wedding of the Lamb has come and his bride has made herself ready.
> Fine linen bright and clean, was given her to wear."
> [Fine linen stands for the righteous acts of the saints.]

We, the body of Christ, have been the betrothed, engaged to Christ upon our salvation. But it is when we all are gathered together in Heaven that we will actually celebrate the wedding feast with our promised love, Jesus Christ. Come quickly Lord Jesus, come quickly. It is through what He has done for us that we can celebrate the truth of who He is.

Saints can be the simple and innocent. They can be sharp in mind and deeply profound of heart. They are the "called out" of our faith, young and not so young, feeble and bereft of heart, mightily strong both in spirit and in resolve. These are God's martyrs and saints.

PASSION FLOWER

INCREDIBLE BEAUTY EXUDES FROM THE PASSION FLOWER WITH ITS
BRILLIANT PURPLE FLOWERS. BLANDINA, MARTYRED SAINT OF OLD,
WE ADHERE TO YOUR PROFESSION OF FAITH AND ADMONISH OURSELVES
FOR NOT BEING AS DELIBERATE AS YOU WERE IN YOUR STUNNING
ALLEGIANCE TO GOD. WE REMEMBER YOU FOR YOUR SACRIFICIAL
PROFESSION OF FAITH.

Blandina

Unknown – A.D. 177

Martyred Slave Girl of Lyon

To know there are actual recorded events of the deaths of martyrs of antiquity shows the tenacity of the saints in encouraging the church to remain faithful through persecution.

This is one such story of a martyred saint of the church, a woman martyr, the first recorded in history. Blandina of France was among the band of Martyrs of Lyons who endured horrific torture and sufferings under the reign of Marcus Aurelius in A.D. 177. These reports were recorded by Eusebius in the book *Historia Ecclesiastes, Volume 2.*

When the Christians began to face the scrutiny of the pagan populace, they created such extreme excitement that whenever they ventured out in public they were harassed and treated with contempt.

During a time when the Imperial Legate [rulers above rulers] was away, the chiliarch, a military commander, and the duumvir, a civil magistrate, threw a number of Christians who had publicly professed their faith into prison. The imprisoned believers were soon brought to trial upon the return of the Imperial Legate. Among the number of Christians held was a master and his slave girl, Blandina, young and frail in body. Because of this her companions feared she would not be able to withstand the torture and remain steadfast for the name of Christ. It was when she was cruelly tortured by the Legate, so much so that the executioners became exhausted, that her fellow believers realized that she was a champion of the faith. The executioners began to wonder "as they did not know what more they could do to her." Still she remained faithful and at every question asked, repeatedly, "I am a Christian, and we commit no wrongdoing."

Every kind of sordid lie began to spread about the Christians in captivity by the heathen slaves who testified against them for fear of torture from their masters. They claimed that when the Christians assembled they resorted to cannibalism and incest. The Legate wanted to bring about confessions from the imprisoned believers. However, when they received orders from Marcus Aurelius allowing the Roman citizens who persisted in the faith to be beheaded for their untoward loyalty to Jesus Christ, they set about to execute those in their prison.

Interrogated in the forum by the provincial governor, those who professed Christ were tortured incessantly all day long, by wild beasts in the amphitheatre. In place of the gladiatorial contests in its many forms, these extreme executions brought lustful pleasure to the heathen crowds that filled the amphitheatres to capacity. They were made a spectacle before the unbelievers. Nevertheless, the just stood firm in their resolve to never give in no matter how horrific the depths of their suffering might be.

Blandina, her master and many men, women and children were sentenced to die by wild beasts in the amphitheatres. With their hope in Jesus Christ beating within their breasts, they resolved to stand strong in the midst of severe persecution and certain death.

The dank prison caused Blandina much discomfort as she lay shaking on the cold, damp, stone floor. The conditions were so terrible that several of her Christian companions died during the night, and their lifeless, pale faces stared at her with eyes wide open. Shutting her eyes to this sight of her fellow prisoners, she cringed as she listened to the sounds of the suffering around her, trying to stifle her own cry of pain and the pounding of her aching heart. A Roman guard appeared at the cell door, and as the metal door scraped open they were descended upon by soldiers who herded them out and into the blinding sunlight of the arena.

Falling, crying and trying to reason what was upon them, the Christian men, women and children were beaten and driven to the center of the amphitheatre. The blood thirsty spectators roared their greeting to the innocent amid curses and shouts of death to the Christians. On a raised platform towering over them stood the Roman governor of Gaul, a laurel wreath crowning his noble head.

The governor held complete authority over the lives of the people and they knew it. Huddling together they squinted in the bright sunlight as they heard him say, "If you would swear an oath by Caesar, I will release you. You will be free to leave this moment if you would but foreswear your belief in this Christ, this Jesus you call God."

When a young man by the name of Vettius stepped forward to speak to the governor, he explained that the Christians were not a threat to Caesar or to anyone at all. All they wanted to do was to live in peace and worship their God. The pagan spectators howled loudly at Vettius' attempt to prove the innocence of the Christians.

The governor ignored him and asked him, "Are you a Christian?"

"I am," Vettius answered loudly, standing confidently before the governor.

Without even looking at the man before him the governor waved for the guards to take him away. Drawing their swords they cut Vettius down where he stood. Then the governor called for Sanctus, a deacon of the church, from the circle of confessors in the arena.

"What is your name?"

"I am a Christian," Sanctus said.

"Are you slave or free?"

"I am a Christian."

The governor was so outraged that he signaled the guards to whip and beat him, but still he answered, "I am a Christian," to everything that the governor asked of him. Then the governor ordered him to be crushed between two red-hot copper plates. He died standing firm in his faith.

Blandina and her fellow sufferers were led back into the prison. All night and through the day the soldiers tormented Blandina. They crushed her limbs upon the rack and pierced her body with daggers. "Curse Christ!" they demanded. "You must tell us all the wicked things the godless do while professing this Christ."

"I am a Christian," Blandina would answer. "We do nothing to be ashamed of."

The soldiers were astonished that she was still alive at the end of a day of torment, and that she was able to draw even one breath was beyond anything they had ever witnessed. "Who are these Christians?" they asked one another. "They go willingly and joyfully to their death."

When dragged into the arena the next day along with several other Christians, Blandina cast her eyes heavenward and prayed aloud, "Father strengthen us as we suffer for the glory of Christ." The crowds raved and screamed for the death of the godless Christians. The beasts tore into the flesh of the believers, but they had been encouraged and heartened by Blandina's prayers to God. The crowd cheered as the wild animals attacked the Christians, but were astounded at the sight of one woman standing in the midst of the slain martyrs. The beast had not touched Blandina, but had torn her fellow sufferers to pieces. The guards carried her back to the prison, but to return a few days later.

On the day she was brought back into the arena, a young Christian boy of fifteen, Ponticius, was led in as well. Blandina urged him to "stand firm" as they were whipped and buffeted about by the soldiers, bloodied and broken, yet resilient in the face of death. The peace of Christ radiated in her face.

"She looked," one eyewitness said, "as if she were invited to a wedding feast, not thrown to the beasts."

Blandina's persecutors became annoyed, frustrated and angry. So infuriated were they by her fortitude that they wrapped a net around her and threw her to a bull that tossed her around the arena. Never in all their time in the arena had they seen a woman withstand such torture. All the pagans marveled at her perseverance during the days of her suffering, and they knew they had never seen anyone, woman or man, last this long in the face of such overwhelming violence. The time had finally come for Blandina's suffering to be through and a soldier reached down and slew her with a sword.

The bodies of the Christians, including those of Blandina, Ponticius and the others, lined the streets of Lyons. While the guards stood constant vigil over the bodies, they were asked why the dead martyrs were not handed over to their loved ones for a decent burial. "So they may have no hope in the resurrection," they answered. "It is this hope that gives them such courage."

For a full six days the bodies lay exposed in the streets for all to see and bear witness. When the six days were complete the soldiers burned the bodies to ashes and scattered the remains in the Rhone River. "These Christians will never rise again. Let's see if they can come to life now." The guard thought that by burning their bodies the power of God would not be able to restore them to life everlasting.

Many Christians in Lyons escaped the persecution and survived to write an account of the martyred believers. They sent the recorded event to the churches throughout the Roman Empire, encouraging them to hold fast to their faith. It was deemed that believers everywhere should not forget Blandina and the Christian martyrs of Lyons and all they had to endure as they stood the test to bear up under suffering and death for Christ. It is with humility and solemn reverence that we remember the martyrs and thank God for their story of encouragement. "Stand firm, dear saints, stand firm."

Scripture Application

"ALL MEN WILL HATE YOU
BECAUSE OF ME, BUT HE
WHO STANDS FIRM TO THE
END WILL BE SAVED."

MARK 13:13

Reflections on Faith for Standing Firm

Have people ever thought you couldn't do a job and you showed them just how well you could do it? Have you ever overcome a difficult situation and amazed yourself with your dedication and resolve?

Picture yourself succeeding in ways that have been impossible for you to imagine. They might be situations that require you to stretch your faith in a variety of ways, like losing weight, quitting smoking, exercising, thinking more positively or reading and studying Scripture.

Determine today that this will be the day that you prayerfully undertake a task that you have been avoiding.

ASTOEMERIA

FRIENDSHIP AND DEVOTION SIGNIFIES THE ASTOEMERIA AS IT BOLDLY
PROCLAIMS ITS BEAUTY IN THE GARDEN. IT IS THROUGH THEIR OWN
DETERMINATION TO STAND TOGETHER IN THEIR PASSION FOR THE LORD
JESUS CHRIST THAT PERPETUA AND FELICITAS DECLARED THEIR ULTIMATE
DEVOTION TO THEIR FAITH. PERPETUA AND FELICITAS MADE THEIR
DECLARATION TO THE WORLD WHEN THEY GAVE THEIR ALL FOR HIM.

Perpetua

A.D. 181 – A.D. 203

Felicitas

Unknown – A.D. 203

Women Martyrs of Lyons

These are the events that were written in the year 202 A.D. concerning the Martyrs of Lyons who were tortured and killed in the amphitheatre of Carthage. The records reveal the agony of the confessors of the faith, the suffering they endured, and the martyrdom they embraced. They testify to the saving power of Jesus Christ and what it meant to give their all for their Savior. These women lived as saints and martyrs of the faith.

Vivia Perpetua, a twenty-two-year-old married mother with a young son and an infant still suckling at the breast, was arrested for confessing Christ as Lord and faced an extremely violent death. Born into a respectable family and liberally educated, Perpetua had a loving mother and father, plus two brothers, one of whom was also a believer in Christ. Among the others that were apprehended were Revocatus, Saturninus, Secundulus and Perpetua's servant Felicitas.

Perpetua's account was recorded by her in a prison diary while she awaited sentencing and death.

"While we were still with the persecutors," she says, "and my father, for the sake of his affection for me, was persisting in seeking to turn me away, and to cast me down from the faith, 'Father,' said I, do you see, let us say, this vessel lying here to be a little pitcher, or something else?' And he said, 'I see it to be so.' And I replied to him, 'Can it be called by any other name than what it is?' And he said, 'No.' 'Neither can I call myself anything else than what I am, a Christian.'

"Then my father, provoked at this saying, threw himself upon me as if he would tear my eyes out. But he only distressed me and went away overcome by the devil's arguments. Then, in a few days after I had been without my father, I gave thanks to the Lord. [The Lord became a source of consolation in the absence of her father.]

"In that same interval of a few days we were baptized, and to the Spirit prescribed that in water of baptism, nothing else was to be sought for bodily endurance. [Within a few days Perpetua's spirit was greatly uplifted through the blessing of water baptism. Her baptism provided a source of comfort for her spirit even though her flesh continued to endure much suffering.]

"After a few days we were taken into the dungeon, and I was very much afraid, because I had never felt such darkness. O terrible day! O the fierce heat of the shock of the soldiery, because of the crowd! I was very unusually distressed by my anxiety for my infant. [Perpetua struggled with the intense heat of the dungeon and the maddening press of the Roman Soldiers at every turn. The most distressful was the ache of her arms for her baby, and the need to nurse him. Her mother's instincts were keenly in tune with her son's need to be at her breast for comfort and nourishment.]

"There were present there Tertius and Pompnius, the blessed deacons who ministered to us and had arranged by means of a gratuity (bribe) that we might be refreshed by being sent out for a few hours into a pleasanter part of the prison. Then going out of the dungeon all attended to their own wants. I suckled my child, which was enfeebled with hunger. In my anxiety for it, I addressed my mother and comforted my brother, and commenced to their care my son. I was languishing because I had seen them languishing on my account. Such solicitude I suffered for many days and I obtained for my infant to remain in the dungeon with me; and forthwith I grew strong and was relieved from distress and anxiety about my infant; and the dungeon became to me as it were a palace, so that I preferred being there to being elsewhere."

Felicitas, who was with child and in the eighth month at the time of her incarceration, was fearful that she would not be selected to suffer martyrdom with the others, since the law prohibited the execution of women who were pregnant. Her heart's desire was to be included with her friends in their suffering for the glory of Christ. Her fellow martyrs were saddened to think that their companion Felicitas would be without them and would have to endure torture and death alone at some future time after her delivery.

Together they all united in prayer, pouring forth their heart to God for their dear sister. Immediately after their prayer, just days before the games were to begin Felicitas went into premature labor, suffering the indignity of a difficult birth in the filth of the prison.

One of the servants of the prison said to her, "You who are in such suffering now, what will you do when you are thrown to the beasts, which you despised when you refused to sacrifice?"

And she replied, "Now it is I that suffer what I suffer; but then there will be another in me, who will suffer for me, because I am about to suffer for Him."

A daughter was born to Felicitas, and she was able to arrange for a Christian woman to take her as her own child.

These torturous narratives concerning Felicitas and those of her fellow martyrs are historic facts and can be found in the recorded document the "Acta." This law was enacted by order of Septimius Severus (193-211) and stated that all imperial subjects were forbidden under severe penalties to become Christians or Jews. The reason only these few were selected lay in the decree that only new converts would be affected by the order. Since these six were recent catechumens (converts) at Carthage, they were seized and cast into prison.

Again in her diary, Perpetua writes:

"And when the day of the exhibition drew near, my father, worn with suffering came in to me, and began to tear out his beard and to throw himself on the earth, and to cast himself down on his face, and to reproach his years, and to utter such words as might move all creation. I grieved for his unhappy old age. He came up to me, saying, 'Have pity my daughter, on my grey hairs. Have pity on your father, if I am worthy to be called a father by you. If with these hands I have brought you up to this flower of your age, if I have preferred you to all your brothers, do not deliver me up to the scorn of men. Have regard to your brothers, have regard to your mother and your aunt, have regard to your son who will not be able to live after you. Lay aside your courage, and do not bring us all to destruction; for none of us will speak in freedom if you should suffer anything.'

"These things said my father in his affection, kissing my hands, and throwing himself at my feet; and with tears he called me not Daughter, but Lady. And I grieved over the grey hairs of my father that he alone of all my family would not rejoice over my passion. And I comforted him, saying 'On that scaffold whatever God will shall happen. For know that we are not placed in our own power, but in that of God.' And he departed from me in sorrow.

"Another day, while we were at dinner, we were suddenly taken away to be heard, and we arrived at the town-hall. At once the rumor spread through the neighborhood of the public place, and an immense number of people were gathered together. We mounted the platform. The rest were interrogated and confessed. Then they came to me. And my father immediately appeared with my boy, and withdrew me from the step, and said in a supplicating tone, 'Have pity on your babe.'

"And Hilarianus the procurator, who had just received the power of life and death in the place of the Procounsul Minucius Timinianus, who was deceased, said, 'Spare the grey hairs of your father; spare the infancy of your boy, offer sacrifice for the wellbeing of the emperors.'

"And I replied, 'I will not do so.'

"Hilarianus said, 'Are you a Christian?'

"And I replied, 'I am a Christian.'

"And as my father stood there to cast me down from the faith, he was ordered by Hilarianus to be thrown down and was beaten with rods. And my father's misfortune grieved me as if I myself had been beaten. I so grieved for his wretched old age. The procurator then delivered judgment on all of us and condemned us to the wild beast, and we went down cheerfully to the dungeon. Then, because my child had been used to receive suck from me and to stay with me in the prison, I sent Pomponius the deacon to my father to ask for the infant, but my father would not give it him. And even as God willed it, the child no longer desired the breast, nor did my breast cause me uneasiness, lest I should be tormented by care for my babe and by the pain of my breast at once."

As the day approached the condemned Christians were transferred to the prison in the camp to ready them for the military games for the pleasure of Emperor Geta on his birthday festival. The jailer Pudens, a soldier, and an assistant overseer of the prison had developed great respect for the prisoners, esteeming them because of the evidence of the great power of

God in them. It was because of his kindness that they had been allowed to see family members and other Christian brethren that they might be refreshed and mutually encouraged. Not to be deterred, Perpetua's father once again tried to convince her to recant her confession.

Secundulus, one of the confessors among them, died before he could offer himself to the beasts, dying not without favor, but with the blessing of his heavenly Father.

Finally the day of their victory shone forth, and the five remaining to be martyred proceeded from the prison into the amphitheatre where Perputua's countenance radiated only joy. A delicate bride of Christ and beloved of God, she cast her gaze from the maddening throng, embracing the moment of triumph over her enemy, Satan.

When they were brought to the gate, they were instructed to put on assigned clothing—men, that of the priests of Saturn, and the women, that of those who were consecrated to Ceres. Perpetua, that noble-minded woman resisted even to the end with constancy. For she said, "We have come thus far of our own accord, for this reason that our liberty might not be restrained. For this reason we have yielded our minds, that we might not do any such thing as this ... we have agreed on this with you." Injustice acknowledged the justice; the tribune yielded to their being brought as simply as they were.

Felicitas rejoiced in the Lord that she had been brought safely through childbirth, so that she might receive the second baptism; from the blood of delivery, to the blood drawn of the gladiator and the wild beasts. Perpetua sang psalms realizing her victory even then and as they came within sight of Hilarianus, by gesture and nod, they began to say to Hilarianus, "Thou judgest us, but God will judge thee."

The pagan mob, overhearing the comments of the three men soon to be martyred, was exasperated and demanded that they first be scourged and tormented as they passed along the *venatores*. They only rejoiced even more for their added affliction. After the scourging the men were set upon by a boar, a bear, and a leopard. The huntsman that provided the boar was gored by that same beast, and died the day after the shows. Satrninus had professed that he wished that he might be thrown to all the beasts that he might wear a more glorious crown. At the beginning of the exhibition, he and Revocatus faced the slashing teeth of the leopard that sought their throats. They barely escaped the leopard with their lives when they came face to face with the bear with its savage eyes and gaping jaws.

Perpetua and Felicitas had been stripped of their clothes and clothed with nets and led forth before the roaring throng who chanted for their blood. The devil had prepared a very fierce cow, provided especially for this purpose. Contrary to the custom of using bulls in the arena, the heifer was used to make a mockery of the female martyrs, making sport of their supposed "weaker sex." But make no mistake, this cow was every bit as deadly as a bull. Its tremendous size and massive strength would utterly destroy the two vulnerable women.

Perpetua's delicate, slender frame and Felicitas' newly delivered body, with breasts still full yearning for her babe's suckling, caused the crowd to shudder at the sight. Both women were recalled and unbound, a tunic draped over them before returning to the arena. Perpetua was led into the arena first, where the beast tossed her in the air causing her to fall on her loins; and when she saw that her tunic had exposed her, she drew it about her middle, more mindful of her modesty than her suffering. Once more they called for her, so she bound up her disheveled hair; for she thought it unbecoming of a martyr to suffer with disheveled hair, lest some might think she was mourning in her glory. As she rose up to suffer once more, she saw Felicitas crushed, and going to her she reached out her hand to her and lifted her up. Standing together it seemed that the populace might be appeased, so they were recalled to the Sanavivarian gate.

Rusticus, who was still a catechumen, kept close to Perpetua. She, as if aroused from sleep, so deeply had she been in the Spirit and in an ecstasy, began to look around her, and to say to the amazement of all, "I cannot tell when we are to be led out to that cow." It was only when she saw the wounds and injury to her body, and in her dress that she understood all that had happened. Recognizing the catechumen and the brother, she addressed them saying, "Stand fast in the faith, and love one another, all of you, and be not offended at my sufferings."

When Saturus was bound on the floor near to a bear, the bear would not come forth from his den. So Saturus was recalled, but when standing before Pudens, the jailer, he said, "Assuredly here I am, as I have promised and foretold, for up to this moment I have felt no beast. And now believe with your whole heart. Lo, I am going forth to that beast, and I shall be destroyed with one bite of the leopard." And immediately at the conclusion of the exhibition he was thrown to the leopard; and with one bite he was bathed with such a quantity of blood that the people shouted out to him as he was returning, the testimony of his second baptism. "Saved and washed, saved and washed."

It is to this final end that the martyrs were called forth before the murderous crowd that eagerly sought to view their last breaths. So the friends in Christ rose on their own accord and went to the place in the arena that the crowd wished to view them; but they first kissed one another that they might consummate their martyrdom with the kiss of peace.

Saturus received the first thrust of the sword, while the rest, silent and immoveable, awaited death. As Perpetua felt the blade of the sword piercing her flesh between her ribs, she cried out loudly in pain. Taking the shaking right hand of the young gladiator, she assisted him by placing the sword at her throat. Even in her suffering she thought of another. The young gladiator who had hesitated in taking her life risked his own, had she not encouraged him to follow through.

Thus the martyrs of Lyons expressed their love for Christ and with their dying breath they paid homage to the King of kings and Lord of lords. Come quickly Lord Jesus, come quickly.

Scripture Application

> "BLESSED ARE YOU WHEN MEN HATE
> YOU, WHEN THEY EXCLUDE YOU AND
> INSULT YOU AND REJECT YOUR NAME
> AS EVIL, BECAUSE OF THE SON OF MAN.
> REJOICE IN THAT DAY AND LEAP FOR
> JOY, BECAUSE GREAT IS YOUR REWARD
> IN HEAVEN. FOR THAT IS HOW THEIR
> FATHERS TREATED THE PROPHETS."
>
> LUKE 6:22-23

Reflection on Faith for Sacrifice:

It would be hard for most of us to imagine suffering and dying for Christ, but the thought of surrendering your child or your loved ones for the sake of Jesus seems unbearable!

What things are you sacrificing to live in faith?

Extreme as it may seem, people die every day all over the world because of their confession of Christ. Have you confessed Christ before man as we are called to do?

Are you dying to the world on a regular basis? Resolve today that you will live each day praying for the persecuted church, and pray that you may be strong if your life is ever required of you because of your faith in Christ.

SEA LAVENDER

THE PURPLE FLOWERS AND GREEN FOLIAGE SEEM TO DECLARE FREEDOM
AND IDENTITY OF SELF TO THOSE WHO WOULD STOP TO GAZE AT THE
BEAUTY IN THIS UNIQUE PLANT IN THE GARDEN. WHAT IS THIS THAT
SEEMS SO STALWART AND DIFFERENT AMONG THE REST? THE REFRAIN IS
THAT OF A SPECIAL CREATION BY THE FATHER, TO GIVE HIM GLORY AND
HONOR. THUS IT WAS FOR OUR TWO MARGARETS AS THEY WITHSTOOD
THE TEMPEST OF HATRED THAT SWIRLED AROUND THEM.

Margaret McLachlan

1622 – 1685

Margaret Wilson

1667 –1685

Martyred Covenant Ladies

During the years 1684 and 1685 persecution against the Covenanters brought terrible suffering to the Lord's people in the West of Scotland. This time was called "The Killing Time," a time when both young and old alike were the scourge of the land. The innocent victims were hunted over moors and mountains and once captured were tortured and slaughtered because of the faith.

The savage ruffians were like devils incarnate as they killed poor souls who might be reading their Bibles or those who were unable to answer their questions. Often times it was a hapless onlooker that, in their own fear, ran from the scene only to be captured themselves because of their proximity.

During a reign of terror as many as eighty people were shot in the fields in cold blood and people met on the highway could simply be shot dead on the spot for being persistent in their rebellion. The Duke of York had openly threatened, saying, "There was no other way of rooting fanaticism out." The ferocity of the persecutors had reached fever pitch as they sought to extinguish the life and faith of those who stood for Christ. Refusing the king's decree to return to the English Church and to abide by his demands to abandon their faith, they were ruthlessly hunted down like wild beasts.

Spiritual decline was spreading across the whole of the British Isles, and the Glasgow assembly of 1610—a church court corrupted by intimidation and bribery—introduced the whole prelatic system of Church government. This system required that all churches would be under the rule of the King of England as he sat as the head of the Church of England.

The Scottish Church had once been filled with the Psalms of the faithful as they worshiped the Lord Jesus Christ with their whole heart, but now even their own had been bribed and corrupted. When the ruling came that only the English Church would serve in ministries, they were forbid to worship as they chose. The whole point of the king's ruling over the Scottish people and the entire country was one of control and not one of faith in God. It had little to do with the worshipping of Christ and much to do with the godless abandonment of the faith altogether. The precious faith of the Scottish people had been crushed and the people who resisted the proclamation were given a death warrant.

There was at this most terrible time in history a farmer by the name of Gilbert Wilson who along with his wife tended to their well-stocked farm and sought to raise their children peaceably. They were conformists to prelacy, and regularly attended the ministry of the curate of Penningham. The government had no quarrel with their agreeable behavior. The Wilson's children were thoughtful concerning the matters of religion and seemed to be drawn to the forbidden faith of the Covenanters. They knew even at a young age the dangers that lay in wait for those who would not conform to the king's Church. They worshipped in hiding for fear of severe reprisal from the king's men and even from their own pagan countrymen. Their ardent attachment to the persecuted faith drew them deeper into their love for Christ and no matter how their parents pleaded with them they would not attend the prelatic ministry parish.

Because of their devotion to Christ and their desire to worship Him in true fashion, they joined with the Covenanters and went into hiding. Escaping into the upper part of Galloway, they sought the desert solitudes as the place to join others in like peril. The children were treated like outlaws and were in danger night and day of being found out and arrested. Their dear parents were unable to help them or supply any of their basic needs or wants for fear of being apprehended. The Wilson children—Margaret, eighteen, Agnes, thirteen and their brother of sixteen—accompanied the other persecuted wanderers, hiding in the caves of Carrick, Nithsdale and Galloway. They sought shelter in the mosses, mountains and other hidden safe places where the dreaded executors might not find them and take their life. They were cold, dirty, hungry and without their parents' natural love and affection. But for them, loving Jesus in the way they were called to worship Him was more important, and they risked it all for His sake.

During this time young Margaret Wilson's father was fined for his children's non-conforming to the prelacy, even though he and his wife were compliant. They were also maligned routinely by soldiers, sometimes as many as a hundred, who would come by his house. Because he was a man of considerable wealth, they looked greedily at him and through envy would maliciously destroy his property. They would take free lodging from the much put upon farmer, harassing him and causing both husband and wife much anguish. Wilson was once one of the most affluent men in that part of the country, but because the soldiers did so much damage to his property, he died destitute. On his passing in what was believed to be 1704 or 1705, his poor widow had to rely on the charity of her friends just to survive into her old age. The soldiers were much like licensed thieves who traveled the countryside preying on innocent people, conformists and non-conformists alike, terrorizing whomever they chose.

It was only a matter of time before Margaret Wilson and her sister Agnes fell into the hands of their persecutors. After hiding in the moors and mountains for some time it appeared that the persecution was lessening a bit and they decided to secretly attempt to visit some of their fellow sufferers. There was a very kind, aged woman, a widow by the name of Margaret McLachlan, whom they greatly respected and loved. Mrs. McLachlan was more than qualified to provide the young girls with confident counsel for the deep trouble they were enduring. Not only was she able to provide sound council, she was able to give them warmth, affection, and comfort they were sorely in need of.

There was a devious man by the name of Patrick Stuart with whom the young Wilson girls were personally acquainted and who seemingly professed to have a deep concern for their welfare. Such was not the case and Stuart betrayed the girls' trust, either for the paltry reward money he would receive or from sheer evilness. It was through a rather devious plan he had devised to give him just cause to turn them into the authorities. Knowing their pious character, he acted the part of a warm friend and invited them to engage in some refreshment. Once happily persuading the unsuspecting sisters, their Judas suggested a toast to the king's health. Knowing full well that they would decline to lift a cup to the king, which they did in all modesty and humbleness, he promptly left them and went directly to the authorities in Wigton. There he lodged a grievous charge against them and gave all the information necessary for their arrest warrant to be made. Naturally soldiers were dispatched for their immediate apprehension and arrest. The girls were then cast into a most horrendous place called "the thieves' hole" where they stayed for a time until they could be moved to the prison. Upon arriving at the prison they were very distraught to find that their dear Mrs. McLachlan was there, having been arrested about the same time they were or shortly thereafter.

The widow of John Mulligan or Millikin, Margaret McLachlan was a woman of virtue and piety. A rather plain woman by man's account, but beautiful in the eyes of those who loved the Lord. She was blameless in her deportment and held a great knowledge of religious teachings, which set her apart and superior to most women of her station. Now having reached the venerable age of seventy years, she had regularly absented herself form hearing the curate of the parish of Kirkinner. Being strictly Presbyterian in her principles she had attended the sermons of the proscribed ministers and offered relief and shelter to her persecuted, nonconforming relations and acquaintances. Through her kindness and love of God, she offered as much as she possibly could to those who were suffering because of the unrelenting press of the persecutors.

Regardless of age or honorable character Mrs. McLachlan's fate had been decided for her highly criminal offense of providing refuge for "the fanatics." It was on the Sabbath day as she was engaged in her worship time in her own home that the soldiers apprehended her in their search for the rebellious Covenanters. Without regard for the sanctity of private worship in one's own home they burst in upon the most holy day of the week, one in which they knew they could catch their prey unaware.

The young Margaret, her sister Agnes, and Mrs. McLachlan were demanded to swear the abjuration oath as a test of their loyalty to the king. This was an oath abjuring a manifesto published by the Society People, or the Cameronians, on November 8, 1684, entitled "The Apologetic Declaration and Admonitory Vindication of the True Presbyterians of the Church of Scotland, especially Intelligencers and Informers." The gist of this Abjuration Oath was that if they did not agree to swear this oath they were charged with high treason—a crime punishable by death.

The three were brought to a formal trial and charged with being at the battle of Bothwell Bridge, at the skirmish of Ayr's Moss, and other uprisings of equal calamity. The whole notion that these three were anywhere near these events was rather ludicrous, seeing as it had been six years previous. The two younger would have been about fifteen and seven, with the elder Margaret still being quite aged and obviously not quite up to rebellious skirmishes on bridges or anywhere else for that matter. There may have been other charges brought against the sufferers, and some may have even been true, but nothing was ever honestly proven. The court again insisted that they swear the abjuration oath, but all of them refused to swear it. This refusal seems to have been the main grounds upon which they were ultimately condemned.

The trial was a mockery of true justice and the jury a shameful sham, so when the sentence was pronounced upon them it was no surprise to those in attendance. Margaret, Agnes and Margaret McLachlan were deemed guilty and sentenced to death by drowning. They were to be tied to stakes fixed within the flood mark in the water of Blednoch, near Wigton, where the sea flows at high water. The date on which this atrocity was to be carried out was May 11, and as they were receiving their sentence the judge commanded that they receive pronouncement on bended knees. All three refused to kneel and because of this they were forcibly caused to kneel until their sentence could be read for all to hear.

Their sentence by no means caused any distress among them, and they rather wore cheerful countenances, filled with uplifting joy to be honored with the call to suffer for the cause of Christ. The friends of the three were not happy, though, and despaired for the loss of three that were much loved and respected. Gilbert Wilson was much afflicted concerning both his daughters' death sentences, and upon his traveling to Edinburgh, he was allowed to purchase the life of his youngest daughter for 100,000 sterling because of her tender age of thirteen. While still in Edinburgh he used every means he could think of to try and save his other daughter. His intercessions were to no avail, and he resigned that his oldest daughter, Margaret, was lost to him forever.

Margaret's friends all tried to persuade her to swear the abjuration oath, and to promise the authorities she would attend the ministries of the curate of the parish in which she lived. It became evident to her friends that under no condition would she surrender her convictions, no matter how impassioned their solicitations.

While imprisoned, Margaret Wilson wrote a long, deeply affecting letter to her family in which she shared her understanding of God's love for her soul. The letter also expressed her sense of resignation in regards to His sovereign disposal where she was concerned. The most vehement statement in her letter centered on her refusal to save her life by swearing the abjuration oath and by engaging to conform to prelacy. Margaret's letter exhibited a manner of thought and solidity of judgment that belied her youthful years and education.

Margaret the elder did not appear to be able to contend with the harshness of prison and was induced to send a petition to the privy council, praying them to recall her sentence of death. In her petition she acknowledged the justice of the sentence, but expressed her more than willing conscience to swear the abjuration oath and attend her parish church regularly.

Gilbert Wilson's plea for his younger daughter's life before the privy council gave them cause to yield to the prayer of this petition and they granted a reprieve to both women, recommending them to the secretaries of state for his majesty's pardon. Alas, even with the reprieve ordered by the privy council the appointed day of execution arrived on May 11, and the two Margarets were led to the place of execution amidst a growing crowd of spectators.

The assembly of onlookers had never witnessed such an unusual sight and congregated in both fascination and horror at what was transpiring before their eyes. A company of soldiers, led by Major Windram, had been assigned to guard and lead the women to the shore and make ready the execution. The stakes were fixed in the sand between the high and low water mark, with Margaret McLachlan placed nearest the advancing tide. The elder Margaret had rallied her courage after her prayerful petition to the privy council and now offered great fortitude and encouragement to her younger counterpart. It was with faithful resolve that she went to her execution knowing that she was soon to draw her last breath, but that she would soon be before Almighty God.

The positioning of the elder Margaret nearest the breaking tide was meant to cause the younger to suffer through mounting terror as she watched as each successive wave swept over her friend. The rising tide covered the aging matron's knees, then her waist, breast, neck, chin and then her mouth, which caused her to spew forth salt water until her entire being was claimed by the sea. As Margaret Wilson watched as the agonies of death claimed her friend, she knew that soon, she too would meet the same fate. During this intense moment one of the crowd, perhaps a guard, heartlessly asked what she thought of the spectacle that lay before her eyes. "What do I see," she answered, "but Christ, in one of His members, wrestling there. Think you that we are the sufferers? No, it is Christ in us; for He sends none a warfare upon their own charges."

When bound to the stake, Margaret Wilson sang several verses of the 25th Psalm. Beginning at the seventh verse:

> *Let not the errors of my youth,*
> *Nor sins remembered be*
> *In mercy for thy goodness' sake,*
> *O Lord remember me.*
> *The Lord is good and gracious*
> *He upright is also*
> *He therefore sinners will instruct*
> *On ways that they should go.*

Through the singing of the beautiful Psalm and the rendering of a portion of the eighth chapter of the Apostle Paul's Epistle to the Romans, Margaret exhibited sublime faith of exquisite proportions. Humbly she relinquished her hold on the world with a radiant countenance, filled with the inner peace and joy that passes all understanding. Engaging in prayer she valiantly fought the surge of water that now began to reach her lips as the struggle for air and preservation of life took command.

The soldiers looking on pretended to show concern for her fight for the ability to lift her head above the increasing waves of the water. They offered to loosen her constraints, which bound her to the stake, if she would but swear the abjuration oath. Loosening the cords, they pulled her from the water, and as soon as she could take in enough fresh air to speak, Major Windram asked if she would pray for the king. Margaret, in all her gentle, Christian character looked directly at the Major: "I wish the salvation of all men and the damnation of none."

A dear friend of hers stood nearby deeply moved by her plight and anxious to save her life. "Margaret, say 'God save the king!'"

With all the composure that she possessed within her being, she quietly, but resolutely replied, "God save him if he will, for it is his salvation I desire."

At this juncture Margaret's friends began to call out to the Major, "Sir, she has said it! She has said it!"

This would not satisfy her executioners, and one who was in authority by the name of Lagg seethed with frustration and anger.

"Damned B----h! We do not want such prayers; tender the oath to her."

Major Windram, standing so close that she could feel his breath on her wet, salted face, demanded that she immediately give the abjuration oath or else she would be given back to the sea.

There was no momentary pause in her reply as she calmly and firmly replied, "I will not; I am one of Christ's children; let me go."

Margaret Wilson, eighteen years of age, preferred to die rather than do what she believed would be a denial of Christ and His truth. The torture of the offer of life was the utmost in her captor's cruelty, pulling her back from the brink of death just to toy with her as a cat does with a mouse. It was with evil, hateful delight that they most deliciously tormented the young confessor of Christ.

Windram's last order concerning his prisoner was to once again lash her to the stake, watching with wicked satisfaction as the undulating sea began to rise above her head. The water continued to rise steadily until the foam and brine covered Margaret completely for what would be the last time.

The two Margarets—Margaret McLachlan and Margaret Wilson—on being taken from the sea, were buried in the churchyard of Wigton.

Scripture Application

"DO NOT BE AFRAID OF WHAT
YOU ARE ABOUT TO SUFFER.
I TELL YOU, THE DEVIL WILL
PUT SOME OF YOU IN PRISON
TO TEST YOU, AND YOU WILL
SUFFER PERSECUTION FOR
TEN DAYS. BE FAITHFUL, EVEN
TO THE POINT OF DEATH,
AND I WILL GIVE YOU THE
CROWN OF LIFE."

REVELATION 2:10

Reflection on Faith for Perseverance:

Do you believe so strongly in your faith that you know you would never waver? What can you do to have integrity in Christ and possess the faith that will provide all the strength you need to meet any circumstance?

The strength of others can help build your resolve to stand strong no matter what the situation. Who among your friends consistently challenges and inspires you in your faith walk? Determine today to surround yourself with such friends when you feel weak.

What character qualities did the two Margarets possess that you would like to develop in your own life?

FLEUR DE LIS

The Fleur de lis has a provocative bloom that commands attention. Could Joan d'Arc be even more beautiful as she stood leading the armies of France against tyranny and oppression? Dear Joan, triumphant, tearful, and compassionate. She will live forever in our hearts and in the presence of King Jesus.

Joan of Arc

1412 – 1431

Maid of Orleans

When one thinks about women saints and martyrs, one name stands above the rest. That name is Joan of Arc of Domremy, France. It is the image of Joan in armor leading the French against the conquering English invaders that thrills both our hearts and minds. Her quest to serve both God and man came as the result of visions she began to have at the tender age of twelve. It was the stirring visions of St. Michael the Archangel (identified in Scripture as the commander of Heaven's armies who waged war against Satan) and Saints Catherine and Margaret (two early Christian martyrs) that set the stage for Joan's later life and the circumstances surrounding her death.

Jehanne d'Arc or Darc, was born in the village of Domremy, France, on January 6, 1412, on the night of the Epiphany. Born the third of five children to Jacques d'Arc and his wife, Isabelle de Vouthon, Joan's humble birth became an important day in France's history. Lord Perceval de Blulainvilliers later claimed that the roosters of the village, "like heralds of a new joy," hailed her birth by crowing long before dawn, as if to announce a different type of dawn. She was christened Jehanne (Joan), apparently after her mother's sister Jehanne Lassois.

Joan's father was a successful farmer who was the owner of nearly thirty acres of cropland, nearly ten acres of pasture and roughly ten acres of forestland. Isabelle, or Isabellete, Joan's mother, was a devout Catholic who along with her husband Jacques raised their three sons, Jacquemin, Jean, Pierre, and two daughters, Joan and her sister Catherine, in piety and faith. Under Isabelle's tutelage her children were instructed to be reverent and obedient in all matters of daily living, especially in the teachings concerning the things of God and the church. The d'Arc family was known by the local villagers as "good, faithful Catholics," and good farmers of reputable, upright living.

Joan's childhood was spent tending her father's herds and roaming the pastures and meadows of the Meuse River valley. By all accounts based on the testimony of people who knew her during her early years, it seems that she was a quiet, serious girl who was quite fastidious in keeping her chores. It was remembered by a childhood friend of hers, Simonin Musnier, that "she helped those who were ill and gave alms to the poor, as I saw, because I was ill when I was a boy and Joan consoled me."

Often times she would sneak off to hear mass or visit a local church or shrine when she should have been working, making this her only "disobedience" to her parents. This rather unusual behavior gave rise to some of the village boys teasing her about being "too pious." Their ideas about Joan were not too far off. She sought to know God in a deeper sense as she listened intensely to the voices that accompanied the visions she had. The voices often came to Joan while in her father's garden, often just before noon, or frequently occurring during the ringing of the church bells at Compline, which called people to prayer (around 9 P.M.). At other times she would experience the visions while walking through the woods on her way to a church or a shrine.

As Joan matured, the visions that once encouraged her as a child to prayer and piety now began to exhort her to carry out the details of the mission given to her by God. During this time Joan appears to have withdrawn from all social life of the village. The village tradition of "Fountains Sunday" was a church tradition that allowed people a break from the Lenten fasting. This time of celebration would be enjoyed by dancing and picnics, with much fun and feasting, but Joan preferred to spend time off by herself. She would visit her beloved churches, especially Notre Dame de Bermont, a small isolated chapel in the middle of the woods above the nearby village of Greux.

During the year of Joan's birth in 1412, France was in the midst of unsteady truce between with England. Two factions of the French Royal family had erupted into a civil war that would inevitably allow the English to re-invade. Count Bernard VII of Armagnac and Duke Charles (for whom Joan would have great affection) led the "Orleanist" or "Armagnac" faction, and their rivals the "Burgundians" were led by Duke John-the-Fearless of Burgundy. Because of the civil war raging in France negotiations to renew the truce with England failed, permitting King Henry V to invade France in August of 1415. The invading Henry revived his family's claim on the French throne and by 1417 the Northern parts of France were conquered. By 1419 the new Burgundian Duke, Philip-the-Good agreed to recognize King Henry V as the legal heir to the French throne. Joan considered Charles of Ponthieu (later known as Charles VII) the rightful successor, the last heir of the Valois dynasty that had ruled France since 1328. This time of war would be known as the 100-year war.

In 1428 the situation became critical, as the English prepared to attack the city of Orleans. It was at this time that Joan responded to God's command to lead an army against the English and the Burgundians, explaining that God had taken pity on the French for the suffering they had endured. So in May of 1428 the "Maid of Orleans" embraced her destiny, traveling to meet with her relative Durand Lassois to convince him to take her to Vaucouleurs to speak with the garrison commander. Lord Robert de Baudricourt, a loyalist to the Armagnacs, refused to speak with Joan, but she was not easily deterred.

When the English Army had laid siege to the city of Orleans, Charles was shaken and disheartened by the dire situation. With his treasury sorely depleted and his once splendid army reduced to an assortment of war weary men, there seemed to be little reason to hope. Conditions could not be worse, and he began to wonder about the validity of his cause, since his own mother had declared him illegitimate in order to deny him access to the throne. Her cooperation with the English was one of many tragic setbacks. Now with Orleans, the last major city defending the heart of his territory facing the grip of an English army, it seemed that all was lost. It was on this impossible note that Baudricourt finally granted permission to Joan, after her third attempt, to meet with Charles accompanied by her escort.

How was it that Joan, a mere girl, was able to convince Baudricourt that he should allow her to speak with Charles? One account says that she proceeded to accurately predict a French defeat near Rouvray, north of Orleans. Baudricourt, upon hearing the news of the defeat, promptly ordered Joan to be escorted through enemy territory to speak with Charles at Chinon. Joan's escorts provided her with men's clothing that served both as a disguise and as a measure of protection.

The male clothing had many protective assets, having many cords that were attached to tunic, trousers and boots. These were an added level of security for the young maiden and the eyewitnesses said she always kept this clothing on and laced tightly when in camp with the soldiers. This was done as a matter of decorum of modesty, but most of all, it was necessary for safety while in the battle fields of masculinity. Joan called herself "La Pucelle" (the maiden or virgin) explaining that she had promised her saints to keep her virginity "for as long as it pleases God," and it is by this nickname that she is usually described in the documents.

Joan was seventeen and her resolute determination to follow God's divine plan for her life and for the sovereignty of France was irretrievably set in motion. Joan arrived at the royal court around March 4, after being on the road for eleven long days, and still had to wait another two days before being brought before King Charles. When she was finally presented to Charles, the Royal commander and bailiff of Orleans recalled that "she presented herself before his Royal majesty with great humility and simplicity, a poor shepherd girl, and said to the king, 'Most illustrious lord Dauphin [i.e., heir to the throne], I have come and am sent in the name of God to bring aid to yourself and to the kingdom.'"

Can you imagine the reaction of Charles to this young girl standing before him with her offer to aid all of France? Indeed it was only through her accounts of a private prayer that he had made the previous November 1 that he was convinced of the true calling of her life. She rightly knew that he had asked

God to aid him in securing his rightful place on the throne and if his actions had caused the people of France to suffer, that it should be he, not them that would bear the consequences. Joan's details of his prayer and her assurance of his legitimate claim to the throne left the king with a most radiant appearance. There were many eyewitnesses to the court at the time and much has been noted about her encounter with King Charles.

Being a wise and thoughtful man, Charles first asked that Joan be examined by a group of theologians in the city of Poitiers about thirty miles to the south of Chinon. There the pro-Armagnac clergy from the University of Paris questioned her for three weeks before they gave their approval. The clergy advised the king that he could grant Joan the titular command of an army, an arrangement that was often made during the medieval period to religious visionaries. It was her ability to hold her own among the learned scholars that earned her the reputation as "another Saint Catherine come down to earth."

Joan's reputation began to spread as she ordered clergyman Jean Erault to record an ultimatum to the English commanders at Orleans. This was to be the first of eleven surviving letters that Joan dictated to scribes during the course of her military campaigns. These letters warned the English that Jesus Christ, the son of Saint Mary, was in support of King Charles VII's claim to the throne and strongly advised them to "go away [back] to England or she will 'drive you out of France.'" The English commanders' only reply came from detaining her messengers, leaving her with little choice but to use more forceful tactics to convince the English to pull their troops from the Loire Valley.

A banner was made with a picture of "Our Savior" holding the world with two angels at the sides on a white background covered with gold fleurs-de-lis for Joan's army. They provided a suit of armor "made exactly for her body" (in the words of one eyewitness), then brought her to the army at Blois, about thirty-five miles southwest of Orleans. It was here that Joan began to shape her troops into an army more in keeping with the holy calling placed on her life. This spiritual transformation would begin with her driving out the prostitutes in the camp, sometimes at sword point, according to one eyewitness. She also required the soldiers to attend church, go to confession, quit swearing, and cease their endless onslaught of looting and harassing the civilian population. One first hand report astonishingly told that she successfully convinced the ruthless mercenary commander Lord Etienne de Vignolles, known as "La Hire," meaning "anger" or "ire," because of his quick temper to visit a priest to confess his sins.

Word soon spread that a "saint" was now leading the army, and men who would have otherwise refused to serve in battle now volunteered for the campaign. This spiritual leadership encouraged and brought focus for the weariness that had weighed heavily on all of France. With Joan as the head of the army, men were inspired and imbued with the sense that at last, God was now on their side.

On May 4, all the troops were finally assembled in Orleans and a few hours later a full assault was led by Joan against an English-held church called Saint Loup, about a mile east of the city. From all surviving accounts of the battle, Joan rallied the army up and over the ramparts, exhorting them by riding up with her banner held high for all to see. The toll of 114 dead English with a capture of forty of their men was a satisfying victory for the army.

Joan's role in each engagement remained the same: she always rode into battle with her banner held high, encouraging her soldiers by daring to face the danger they themselves encountered. Joan consistently refused to carry a sword because she did not want to harm anyone, a truth that sometimes escapes pictures in history books, but a fact that both sides reported over and over again. With the "Maid of Orleans" at the head of France's army, a surge of new enthusiasm permeated the troops and the possibility of victory began to build in their hearts and souls.

Joan issued her final ultimatum to the English by having an archer send a note by arrow, rather than losing another messenger to the enemy. On May 6, another attack was made against a fortified monastery called the Bastille des Augustins, which controlled the southern approach to a pair of towers called Les Tourelles, which stood at the end of Orleans' bridge. A church to the east called Jean-le-Blanc was near where the English had been bombarding the city with one of their largest cannons, "le Passe-volant." The English were driven from the church and then Saint Joan, leading the charge, advanced against the monastery with "La Hire" swiftly riding by her side. The fortress was overrun successfully with few casualties, placing the advancing troops in striking range of Les Tourelles for next morning's assault.

Early the next day as they stormed the towers, Joan was wounded by an arrow while helping a soldier with the placement of a scaling ladder. For the rest of the day's fighting she stayed behind the actual battle area, only returning to the field near dusk in order to encourage the discouraged and demoralized troops. With her ability to muster the soldiers into action she challenged them to yet another battle before the day was through. With one more skirmish in their blood they were able to roust the English into abandoning the siege. This last surge of attack proved decisive as the very next day the English moved their troops off to Meung-Sur- Loire and other positions along the river.

This battle at Orleans proved to be the English army's last hold on the city. Their defeat came about because of Joan's spirited ability to rally her troops to victory, enabling Charles to soon be anointed as King Charles VII, rightful heir to the throne of France. Because of the lifting of the siege, many prominent figures offered their support to Charles and promised to send troops to his aid. The Archbishop of Embrun wrote a treatise (June 1492) declaring Joan to be divinely inspired, and advised Charles to consult with her on matters concerning the war.

In an account by Eberhardt von Windecken he describes the meeting of Charles and Joan at Loches: "Then the young girl bowed her head before the king as much as she could and the king immediately had her raise it again; and one would have thought that he would have kissed her from the joy that he experienced." Joan was able to convince the Dauphin to take an army north to Reims to be crowned, as custom required. Because Reims lay deep within enemy held territory, this was no easy task.

Charles had to set the Royal army to clear out the remaining English with the Duke of Alencon being given command of the campaign. Joan was included in the battle carrying her banner up front with the troops, encouraging them to storm the ramparts by shouting: "Friends, friends, up! Up! Our Lord has condemned the English." Even when hit in the helmet by a large stone and knocked down, she valiantly rose to continue to encourage and inspire the courageous men. The English were driven back across Jargeaus' bridge, and the fortifications were taken with the survivor's surrendering to the French army.

The next day, the English reinforced their troops and rode northward in an effort to make it back to more secure territory. Goaded forward by Joan, the French army pursued their enemy, engaging them in a clash just to the south of Patay.

A rapid cavalry charge led by La Hire and other nobles of the vanguard overran a line of 500 English Archers. After this severe trouncing the English heralds announced their losses at 2,200 men, compared to only three casualties for the French—the reverse of so many other battles during that war.

Charles decided to execute the plans to travel to Rheims for his coronation after this major victory and letters were dispatched to various cities and dignitaries requesting that they send representatives to the coronation. News of the French armies' amazing victories spread throughout the country and many opposing factions to Charles decided to support his cause. With letters that Joan personally sent out declaring "with the help of King Jesus" Charles would claim all of the towns within his inheritance regardless of their wishes. Soon they had reached Chalons-sur-Marnne to the north, which opened its gates to the advancing army with little resistance.

Joan counseled Charles to "advance boldly." As she promised he was now poised to receive the crown that had been denied him years earlier. Charles' holy anointing took place with Joan standing next to her Dauphin, her banner held firmly in her hand, the other quietly wiping away her tears. According to one 15th century source who described the scene: after Charles was crowned, Joan "wept many tears and said, 'Noble king, now is accomplished the pleasure of God, who wished me to lift the siege of Orleans, and to bring you to this city of Reims to receive your holy anointing, to show that you are the true king, and the one to whom the kingdom of France should belong.'" It adds: "All those who saw her were moved to great compassion."

The coronation of Charles took place on July 17, and the Duke of Burgundy was very visibly missing. Joan immediately sent a letter asking why he failed to show up for the ceremony.

She admonished him and proposed that he and Charles should "make a good firm lasting peace. Pardon each other completely and willingly as loyal Christians should do, and if it should please you to make war, go against the Saracens." [The Islamic Saracens, frequently at war with Christendom, were one of her preferred targets for legitimate military action.] The Duke's emissaries had arrived in Reims on the day of the coronation with the full intent of beginning negotiations with the king. This only resulted in a fifteen-day truce being declared, which only served to give the English and Burgundians time to regroup. Certainly not the "good, firm, lasting peace" that Joan wanted.

Joan's heart was one of peace, not war, and she was quoted as saying that she now hoped that God would permit her to return to her family's home. This unfortunately was not to be, as Charles made the rounds of the various cities seeking their loyalty and allegiance. There were more skirmishes, battles and campaigns for the French army to contend with, and Joan was leading the charge against the English to try and draw them out. Talks of a peace conference for the spring swirled about amid and between the battles although documents show that the English were planning to launch an offensive around the same time.

With Charles remaining at Compiegne, Joan and the Duke of Alencon prepared a campaign with a body of troops to advance against Paris. They made their way to the region around Paris, arriving at St. Denis with the intention of sending out skirmishers "up to the gates of Paris" over the next several days. As Joan was trying to find a way for her troops to cross the city's inner moat, she was hit in the thigh by a crossbow dart and carried back against her will, all the while urging on another assault. No other attack would be forthcoming, though, and the troops joined King Charles who had now arrived at St. Denis.

The Duke of Alencon had ordered a bridge to be constructed in order to once again attempt an assault on Paris. The king would have none of it and commanded that the bridge be destroyed and the troops withdrawn.

The discouraged men marched back to the Loire and eventually they were disbanded. Perceval de Cagny, the Duke of Alencon's squire and chronicler summed up this event with the terse and bitter statement: "And thus was broken the will of the maiden and the king's army." He and other soldier's felt the same despondent sentiments regarding the decisions made by the king's counselors and blamed them for fatally undermining Joan's successes. Each commander was then dispersed to his own estate, or former areas of operation. When the Duke of Alencon requested that Joan d' Arc join his campaign into Normandy, the royal court refused.

Joan spent time in various residences of the royal court until the next military venture. Joan's squire and bodyguard remembered that the initial assault was a failure with the soldiers in full retreat except for Joan and a handful of men. She was ordered to fall back, but she would not, declaring that she had "fifty-thousand" troops with her and shouted for the army to bring up bundles for filling in the town's moat. Initiating a new assault she took the town "without much resistance." Joan sent out letters to nearby cities asking for them to donate supplies and received two bundles of arrows, two hundredweight of saltpeter, and an equal amount of sulfur. The next siege at La Charite was an unparalleled failure: the chilly weather had arrived for the fall; the army retained "few men"; and the royal court seemed to have abandoned any and all support for Joan's efforts and the support of her troops. Without food supplies or money, there was little hope to keep the army's already flagging spirits buoyed. After another month of struggling along without supplies, the army disbanded. Joan refused to give up, and once again sent out letters, this time to promise the citizens of Rheims that she would aid them in the event of a siege.

Surviving the winter Joan of Arc took the field again in late March or April with her small group that included her brother Pierre, her confessor Friar Jean Pasquerel, her bodyguard Jean d'Aulon, and a few other faithful. They were escorted by an Italian band of 200 merceneraies led by Bartolomew Baretta and they headed for the town of Lagny-sur-Marne where they were putting up a fight against the English. On Easter Sunday, April 22, she arrived at Meun where, as she would later say, her saints had revealed to her that she would be captured "before Saint John's Day" (June 24). Capture and betrayal were her greatest fears, which she stated at many points and times.

On May 6 Charles finally admitted that his counselors and royal court had been manipulated by the duke, "who has diverted and deceived us by truces and otherwise," as Charles wrote in a letter on that date. When Joan learned that the duke had lay siege to the town of Compiegne she refused to let this courageous city in its defiance fall unaided. So, reinforced with 300 to 400 additional troops, Joan and her small army slipped into Compiegne at sunrise. As she prayed in one of Compiegne's churches that morning she was much troubled in spirit. A group of children nearby, curiously watched as she prayed, realizing that this maid was much in need. One of the young boys provided a statement later in life when he was a grown man recounting that she told the children to "pray for me, for I have been betrayed."

Joan was leading a sortie against the enemy camp at Margny later that day when her troops were ambushed by Burgundian forces concealed behind a hill called the Mont-de-Clairoix. Her decision to stay with the rearguard during the retreat was unfortunate as she and her soldiers became trapped outside the city and pinned up against the river when the drawbridge was prematurely raised behind them. As the Burgundian soldiers drew around her, demanding her surrender, she adamantly refused and was dragged off her horse by an enemy archer. The Armagnac's were devastated by Joan's capture, while the Burgundians and English were ecstatic, "overjoyed more so than if they had taken 500 combatants, for they had never feared or dreaded any other commander…as much as they had always feared the maiden up until that day."

Many efforts were made to ransom Joan of Arc from her captors and her men "were doing everything in their power" to try and get her back. It may never be known who betrayed the maiden. Some believed Guillaume de Flavy, the garrison commander of Compiegne was a traitor. Others looked to the royal court with its divided factions as another possibility. King Charles VII was not perceived as guilty, however, nor did he abandon her, as is so often claimed, according to the archives of the Morosini, who were in contact with the royal court. The Burgundians were actually demanded to return Joan in exchange for the usual ransom, with promised threats to treat the Burgundian prisoners with the same measure of treatment meted out to Joan. None of these attempts were successful and they refused to ransom the Maid of Orleans.

Joan languished as a prisoner at the chateau of Beaurevoir for four months and then was transferred to the English in exchange for 10,000 livres. This was the standard procedure common in other cases of prisoner transfers between members of the same side. Pierre Cauchon, who had been successfully retained to organize a previous legal murder for the Anglo-Burgundian faction, was given the task of maneuvering an Inquisitorial trial against Joan. Great pains were taken by the English government in their documentation of all payments made to cover the costs of obtaining Joan and the reward given to various judges and assessors who took part in her trial. Later testimony revealed that the English conducted the proceedings for the sheer purpose of revenge rather than out of any genuine belief that the young girl was an actual heretic.

The English seat of government resided in Rouen, and although Inquisitorial procedures required all suspects to be held in a church-run prison, Joan was kept in the fortress of Crotoy, a secular, military prison with English soldiers as guards. Eyewitness accounts state that for this reason Joan continued to wear her tunic and pants, perhaps two layers of such pants, both attached to the tunic with over two dozen cords to bind them securely. This was her only protection against advances made by the guards. Strangely enough the Inquisitors used this against her charging that it violated the prohibition against cross-dressing. Joan pleaded with Cauchon to transfer her to a church sanctioned prison with only women to guard her, but this was to no avail.

The tribunal usually called forth many witnesses in their hearings against the accused, but Joan was the only witness allowed to testify. They tried to manipulate her and persuade her to give statements that were out and out lies. Subtle half truths were leveled against Joan by Cauchon and his associates, using vague theological arguments that under normal tribunal procedures would be considered null and void. The accused was allowed to appeal to the pope and on all of the eyewitnesses' accounts, Joan repeatedly asked for this request to be honored, as well as a fair trial with non-partisan judges as the law required. All of her earnest pleadings fell on deaf ears that refused to consider her distress and her dignified right to a fair and impartial court hearing.

Though Joan had the medieval ecclesiastic law on her side the tribunal would not honor or abide by any of the rules that governed the proceedings. They knew she had submitted herself to the papacy and the Council of Basel, but they chose to leave out her statements concerning her very submission to the authority of the Church. They even attempted to link her to witchcraft early in the trial, claiming that her banner was endowed with "magical" powers. One of the other outrageous claims was that she allegedly poured hot wax on the heads of little children. All of these accusations were eventually dropped before the formal charges were finally solidified on April 5. Cauchon tried to further discredit Joan by objecting to her use of the "Jesus-Mary" slogan, which was used by the Dominicans who, for the most part, ran the Inquistorial courts. This argument was paradoxical and didn't seem to make a lot of sense, but then nothing in her trial made much sense. They even went so far as to say that her saints were really "demons," despite the transcript's own description that they had counseled her to "go regularly to church" and maintain her virginity.

The final charge brought against Joan is exasperating to the heart and one wonders how the murder of this young girl could have been allowed to happen. Cauchon brought the charge of "cross-dressing" against Joan and used this to solidify her conviction. Cross-dressing! This flimsy charge shows the true lack of character this man actually had—a shame for someone who was supposed to be an ambassador of Christ.

After being relentlessly badgered about her manner of clothing, Joan reluctantly agreed to wear a dress. Her guards immediately increased their efforts to rape her, including "a great English lord" according to the many reputable eyewitnesses to the court. The guards in their frustration eventually took away her dress altogether, firing up a heated argument between Joan and the guards "which lasted till noon" according to the court, bailiff Jean Massieu. This shameful and humiliating action left no other recourse for Joan but to don the old male clothing that she had been forbidden to wear. This provided Cauchon with the ability to charge her a "relapsed heretic" and condemn her to death. All of the eyewitnesses reported that Cauchon promptly strode out of the prison and exclaimed to the Earl of Warwick and other English commanders waiting outside: "Farewell, be of good cheer, it is done!" stating the fact that he had cleverly orchestrated the trap the guards had set for her.

During her trial Joan listened calmly as the sentence was read to her, but when she gave her own address she broke down into weeping. Forgiving her accusers through tears that coursed down her face, she asked only that they pray for her. The judges and assessors wept quietly, while even some of the English officials and soldiers openly sobbed by the end of her discourse. Not all were duly moved by Joan's heartbreaking rendering and some brazen, impatient soldiers became frustrated. One such soldier sarcastically shouted to the bailiff, "What, priest, are you going to make us wait here until dinner?" It was then that the executioner was ordered to "do your duty."

Joan d'Arc, the Maid of Orleans, was brought out and tied to a tall pillar well above the crowd, who pressed forward to get a better glimpse of the heretic. She asked for a cross and an English soldier moved by compassion attempted to make a small one out of wood. Finally a crucifix was brought from a nearby church. While the glowing red embers grew into raging, hot flames, Friar Martin Ladvenu held it up for her to see. The eyewitnesses recalled that Joan repeatedly screamed "in a loud voice the holy name of Jesus, and implored and invoked without ceasing the aid of the saints of Paradise." The torture of the ravaging flames sought her life; the English sought to crush her allegiance to the king; the Burgundians sought to extinguish her legend; but no one, no one, could steal Joan's soul, for that belonged to King Jesus forever and ever. With her last breath she vowed her love for her champion, Jesus, and with that her head dropped, and it was over—at least for this life. The "Flower of France" was now safe in her Savior's arms, her work complete, her job well done. Now was this sweet maid's time of rest.

There was great agitation from the Secretary to the King of England, Jean Tressard, who exclaimed, "We are ruined, for a good and holy person was burned. The Bishop of Therouanne, brother of the same John of Luxembourg whose troops had captured Joan, and the Cardinal of England himself, wept bitterly. Joan's executioner, Geoffroy Therage, confessed to Martin Ladvenu and Iambart de la Pierre afterwards, saying that "he had a great fear of being damned, (as) he had burned a saint."

The English would not be driven from Rouen until November of 1449, and only then would the slow process of appealing the case be initiated. Eventually Cauchon and the other judges were discredited and Joan's case overturned, having been convicted illegally by a corrupt court operating in a spirit of "manifest malice against the Roman Catholic Church, and indeed heresy." They described Joan as a martyr, thereby paving the way for her eventual beatification in 1909 and canonization as a saint in 1920.

One traditional telling of Joan's death at the stake relates that after the burning of the Maid of Orleans, only her heart remained in the ashes. Indeed, Joan d' Arc's heart still remains with us to this very day.

Scripture Application

> "I CONSIDER MY LIFE WORTH
> NOTHING TO ME, IF ONLY I
> MAY FINISH THE RACE AND
> COMPLETE THE TASK THE LORD
> JESUS HAS GIVEN ME."
>
> ACTS 20:24

Reflections on Faith for Sacrificial Living:

Do you know that God has blessed you with a particular mission in life? A sacrificial calling may not always be easy for you to accept and might make you a bit fearful.

What tasks do you feel too weak for? Why? Remember, His strength is made perfect in our weakness. If the Lord has called you for a particular service He will give you the strength to achieve it.

The enemy will confront you at the threshold of any great work you do for God. How do you react when you feel under enemy attack? Stay encouraged, the Lord is your banner and shield as you as fight the good fight for His glory!

WHITE ROSE

THE WHITE ROSE IS RESILIENT IN SPITE OF ADVERSE CONDITIONS
THAT WOULD KEEP IT FROM BLOOMING IN THE GARDEN. THIS FLOWER
PROCLAIMS BEAUTY, PURITY AND HOPE. SOPHIE SCHOLL, SO YOUNG, SO
FULL OF THE ENJOYMENT OF LIFE, STOOD IN THE HOPE OF GOD WHILE
GIVING HER LIFE FOR HIS GLORY.

Sophie Scholl

1921 – 1943

World War II Martyr

When we think of martyrs we invariably remember those who perished in the first century under the unrestrained madness of Nero or of other ancient times. But persecution and martyrdom is with us in this present age with Christians being imprisoned and murdered daily throughout the world. One such martyr lived during the insanity of Adolph Hitler in the midst of the extreme upheaval of Nazi Germany.

Sophie Scholl was a 21-year-old University of Munich student who was actively involved in an organization with other young people that opposed Hitler and his annihilators. She and her brother Hans operated within a group known as "The White Rose," a non-violent resistance movement that distributed anti-war leaflets. Sophie's story, as well as that of her brother Hans and others in "The White Rose" stands as a testament to the fortitude and love they had for their Savior Jesus Christ. Their Christian faith propelled them forward to face the ignoble giants of evil that dominated Europe and the world. Through their youthful exuberance for righteousness and truth they fought the oppressive forces that were extinguishing millions of innocent "undesirables." Whether they were the despised Jews, the mentally ill, the disabled and other supposed burdens of their superior society, the Nazi edict was to kill and destroy.

Sophia Magdalena Scholl was born on May 9, 1921 in Foctehberg am Kocher where her father served as mayor. The fourth of five children, Sophia thrived in a family that embraced God and salvation through Jesus Christ. As members of a Lutheran church the Scholl family's faith was everything. Obeying the dictates of the heart meant, according to her father's oft repeated statement, "What I want for you is to live in uprightness and freedom of spirit, no matter how difficult that proves to be." Sophie and her older brother Hans lived out this family motto in all they did, believing that integrity and living out one's beliefs were imperative.

Sophie began school at age seven when she found learning easy and her childhood carefree. The family moved twice, once in 1930 to Ludwigsburg, and then again in 1932 to Ulm where her father had a business consulting office. By the age of twelve, Sophie entered a secondary school for girls and was required to join the Bund Deutscher Madel (League of German Girls). At first she was very enthusiastic about being a member along with her classmates, but she soon grew critical of the organization's governmental ideals. Scholl was keenly aware of her father's dissenting political views, as well as those of her friends and teachers. In fact it was the political attitude of others that determined whether or not she would choose to be friends with them. In 1937 her brothers and friends had been arrested for taking part in the German Youth Movement and it had an extremely lasting impression on her.

Sophie had developed a somewhat avant-garde approach to life and made friends with several so-called "degenerate" artists. She had an artistic flair, loving to draw and paint, developing a growing interest in philosophy and theology. Her passion for art and her profound faith helped her cope in her country's fall into Fascist National Socialism.

Sophie also had a fondness for children and after graduating from secondary school, she became a kindergarten teacher at the Frobel Institute in Ulm-Soflingen. It was also her hope that the government would recognize her teaching as an alternative to serving in the Reichsarbeitsdienst (National Labor Service), which was required in order to be admitted to the University. Unfortunately this was not to be the case, and in 1941 she began to serve as a nursery school teacher through the auxiliary war service. The ugly truth of the political situation that she was in prompted her to begin practicing passive resistance.

Enrolling in the University of Munich in May of 1942, Sophie chose biology and philosophy as her main courses of study. It was through her brother Hans, who was a medical student there, that she was introduced to his friends who shared the same political views. It wasn't just politics that drew Sophie to this set of new friends but their mutual love of art, music, literature, philosophy and theology. Of course there was also all the fun they had together hiking in the mountains, skiing, and swimming. They were full of youthful energy and zest for life, often attending plays, concerts and lectures as well as all the other exciting ventures they enjoyed together.

Sophie continued to meet new friends, coming in contact with a number of artists, writers and philosophers who became important contacts for her. Theodor Haecker and Carl Muth became particularly close and they spent countless hours together pondering how the individual must act under a dictatorship. In 1942 Sophie's father was serving time in prison for a critical remark he made about Hitler to an employee. It was during this same time that Sophie had to do war service in a metallurgical plant in Ulm during her summer vacation.

During the early summer of 1942 six anti-Nazi Third Reich political resistance leaflets began to circulate. These leaflets had been co-authored by three young men: Willi Graf, Christoph Probst, and Sophie's brother Hans Scholl. They called themselves "The White Rose," which Hans Scholl under interrogation revealed had come from a Spanish novel he had read. *The White Rose*, a novel about peasant exploitation in Mexico, had been published in Berlin in 1931 by the German author B. Traven, who had also written *The Treasure of the Sierra Madre*. The white rose also symbolized purity and innocence in the face of evil. The organization was influenced by a variety of youth movements that Hans Scholl, Sophie and their friends had belonged to. The organizations left deep-seated impressions on all the young people, and the group as a whole were profoundly influenced by their Christian beliefs. The leaflets instructed the Germans to passively resist the Nazis, knowing the evil and deadly force they could use against their victims. The young men had witnessed the horrifying atrocities committed by German soldiers on the western front. The shocking vision of naked Jews being shot while in a pit had sent their heads reeling in disbelief.

Sophie had not been a co-author of the leaflets, contrary to speculation. Her brother purposely tried to protect her from any knowledge of their covert operation, but as soon as she discovered his activities she joined him. Her involvement in the group became invaluable and as a female she was less likely to be stopped by the SS.

The leaflets quoted extensively from the Bible, Aristotle and Novalis, as well as Goethe and Schiller. The leaflets appealed to what the group considered the "German Intelligentsia," those who would naturally oppose the Nazi regime. At first they sent out mailings from cities in Bavaria and Austria, believing that southern Germany would accept their message against the military in a more receptive way. The young men in the group were called to active military service at the end of 1942 during their academic break, and upon their return in January 1943 operations began once more. The group was able to produce between 6,000 and 9,000 copies of their fifth leaflet, "Appeal to all Germans!" which was distributed via courier runs to many cities (where they were mailed.)

The leaflets were all produced on a hand-operated duplicating machine. The "publishing" group was intent on achieving its goal, no matter how difficult, to reach the German people with the truth about Hitler and Nazism. The main author of the leaflets was Hans Scholl, who was embellished upon by Kurt Huber. Together they wrote dire warnings that Hitler was leading Germany into the abyss and with the gathering might of the Allies, defeat was now certain. Readers were urged to "Support the resistance movement!" in the struggle for "Freedom of speech, freedom of religion, and protection of the individual citizen from the arbitrary action of criminal dictator-states." These were the principles that would form "the foundations of the new Europe."

Sophie's heart was to stop the slaughter of the innocent Jews, the young soldiers forced to fight for Hitler's war, and others who fell prey to the Nazi killing machine. She was always willing to do whatever it took to get the message out to the people of Germany. To try and divert attention away from herself she bought stamps and paper at different places, putting herself in danger each time she acted on behalf of The White Rose. Perhaps Sophie, her brother and the others were idealistic and naïve, but they were truly brave in facing the insurmountable terrors of their day.

To better understand how frightening it was to live during this time in history we can look at some of the details that occurred during Sophie's life: Hitler was elected Chancellor of Germany in 1933. In the beginning there was hope that he would bring national pride to the people of Germany, but by 1935 The Nuremberg Laws had demanded expulsion of anyone who was not Aryan, declaring Jews as non-citizens. The international press had begun to report beatings in the streets, so Hitler moved the arena of cruelty away from cities to concentration camps. On November 9, 1938, 30,000 Jews were beaten and arrested, and storm troops burned 191 synagogues on Kristallnacht, "the night for the broken windows," causing 20,000 Jews to flee to the countryside.

This was just the beginning of the nightmare for Germany and the members of The White Rose. Alexander Schmorell had been a member of the army, but when he was asked to swear an oath to Hitler, he asked to be discharged. After serving as a medical orderly in Yugoslavia, Willi Graf turned to passive resistance like the others. When assigned to the Second Student's Company in Munich he met Sophie, Hans, Alexander, Christoph, and Jurgen. Christoph was the only one who was married in the group with young children, so the others did their best to protect him, for the sake of his family.

The first leaflet printed began with the heading: Leaflets of The White Rose. It said: "Nothing is so unworthy of a nation as allowing itself to be governed without opposition by a clique that has yielded to base instinct.... Western civilization must defend itself against fascism and offer passive resistance, before the nation's last young man has given his blood on some battlefield."

Leaflet number two stated: "Since the conquest of Poland, 300,000 Jews have been murdered, a crime against human dignity.... Germans encourage fascist criminals if no chord within them cries out at the sight of such deeds. An end in terror is preferable to terror without end."

Leaflet number three demanded: "Sabotage in armament plants, newspapers, public ceremonies, and of the National Socialist Party.... Convince the lower classes of the senselessness of continuing the war; where we face spiritual enslavement at the hands of National Socialists."

In the fourth leaflet they implored: "I ask you as a Christian whether you hesitate in hope that someone else will raise his arm in your defense?... For Hitler and his followers no punishment is commensurate with their crimes."

When the German's were defeated at Stalingrad in 1943, and Roosevelt demanded unconditional surrender for the Axis powers, an allied invasion was just weeks away. It was on that very night that Hans, Willi, and Alex painted "Down with Hitler," "Freedom" and crossed out swastikas on buildings in Munich.

Not only were these brave students involved in the resistance movement, but their philosophy professor, Kurt Huber, upon learning of the shocking atrocities committed by the state in Germany decided to help work on the final White Rose leaflets. His indignation of such mind-numbing crimes also motivated him to lecture on taboo subjects, such as the writings of the Jewish philosopher Spinoza.

Each leaflet spoke harshly against Hitler, but with each new publication the condemnation grew more critical and more pronounced. They also charged the German people with not speaking out against the mounting terror.

The fifth leaflet challenged: "Hitler is leading the German people into the abyss. Blindly they follow their seducers into ruin.... Are we to be forever a nation which is hated and rejected by all mankind?"

The heated language in each new leaflet caused the Gestapo to step up their efforts in finding the instigators, arresting anyone who appeared even slightly suspicious. It was at this time that Sophie and Hans would deliver the last of The White Rose pamphlets. Brother and sister brought a suitcase of the last leaflets written by Professor Huber to the University and left them in the corridors for the students to discover and read. Hurrying to deliver them before the students flooded the halls on their upcoming break, Hans and Sophie noticed that they had left some of the copies remaining in the suitcase. Deciding it would be a pity not to distribute them they returned to the atrium and climbed the staircase to the top floor. Acting on impulse Sophie flung the last remaining leaflets over the banister into the air where they cascaded to the first floor under the surprised eyes of the university custodian Jakob Schmid.

The police were promptly called and it didn't take long before the Scholls were apprehended and placed under arrest. Not long after, the remaining active members of The White Rose and anyone remotely associated with them were brought in by the Gestapo for interrogation.

It was Sophie, Hans and Probst that were the first to be interrogated and placed on trial before the Volksgerichtshop—the people's court. This court was used to try people for crimes of a political nature, especially crimes against the Nazi German state and enemies of Hitler. In February 22, 1943, the three were found guilty and sentenced to death. Hans and Sophie were able to say goodbye to their parents. Sophie's mother told her daughter to remember Jesus, to which Sophie replied, "You too Mama." Sophie prayed while in her cell and had an opportunity to have a member of the clergy come to see her and pray with her for continued strength. They were all courageous, strong and filled with God's love for the suffering of mankind.

Sophie Scholl, Hans Scholl, and Christoph Probst were all beheaded at the guillotine on the same day as their sentencing. The last words of Hans Scholl were, "Es lebe die Freiheit!" (Long live freedom!)

Sophie's last words are thought to have been, "God, you are my refuge into eternity." The film *Sofie Scholl: The Last Days* shows her last words as being "The sun still shines." Other last words attributed to Sophie are "your heads will fall as well," although there is some dispute over whether Sophie or Hans actually made this statement.

The other White Rose Members Alexander Schmorell and Kurt Huber were beheaded on July 13, 1943, and Willi Graf on October 12, 1943. The friends and colleagues of The White Rose, who helped in the preparation and distribution of the leaflets and helped collect money for the widow and young children of Probst, were caught and sentenced to prison terms ranging from six months to ten years.

In memory of these brave young people, Germany named two hundred schools after the Scholls. Their legacy can be read about in books and viewed in several movies that detail their heroism, so it is critical that we never forget the sacrifice they so selflessly made. They were as David, standing up against Goliath, a supposedly weak, ineffective youth that toppled the enemy with one smooth stone. That stone was faith, and their collective hearts beat with the truth of their Savior Jesus Christ.

Lord, may we live as the champions of The White Rose did, and may we shine as radiantly in the sun as your precious Sophie did in her time of trial on this earth. Amen.

Scripture Application

> I WILL VERY GLADLY SPEND
> AND BE SPENT FOR
> YOUR SOULS.
>
> 2 CORINTHIANS 12:15

Reflections on Faithful Resistance:

Sophie and Hans were involved in passive resistance. Just what does that mean to us in our lives today? How can we resist involvement in activities that might lead us into sinful behavior?

What should we as Christians do when we're aware of events in society that harm others, trample human dignity or bar others from the basic tenants of life and faith?

How can silence be a curse to the world when God would have us speak out truth and righteousness, sometimes at a high personal cost? Determine today that you will stand in the gap for the oppressed, fight the cause of righteousness and always surrender your will for the service of others less fortunate.

THE LITTLE RED ROSE

THIS LITTLE FLOWER IS SO VERY BEAUTIFUL IN MANY VARIED WAYS, BUT
IT DOES NOT SEEK TO BE NOTICED. SIMILARLY, SAINT THERESE OF "THE
LITTLE WAY" SOUGHT TO HELP THOSE AROUND HER THROUGH PRAYER.
WE REMEMBER THIS YOUNG WOMAN FOR HER SWEET CHILDLIKE SPIRIT
AND HER TENDER HEART OF SERVICE.

Saint Therese of Lisieux

1873 – 1897

"The Little Flower"

The story of St. Therese of Lisieux, a Carmelite nun, is a sweet one that encourages a lifestyle of simplicity. I have always been intrigued with Therese and her "little way" and on reading about her life have been moved by her devotion to God.

Louis Martin and his wife Azelie-Marie Guerin had already produced eight children when their daughter Therese was born on January 2, 1873 in Alcon, France. Even though they had a number of children, there was always room for more in their hearts, and little Therese was welcomed by her siblings with open arms. Similar to many large families during that era, the Martin family experienced loss. They would only see five of their eight children live to adulthood.

Therese was a precocious and sensitive child and when her mother died at the age of four she was babied by her father and older sisters. As a result of this over-exuberant nurturing, Therese grew up in a spirit of wanting and needing everything. In fact she was expectant in her demands, knowing that her family would seek to placate her and meet her requests. Her sisters were not always pleased with this behavior, but because she was the baby they always gave into her whims.

Therese's father, Louis Martin had moved his surviving five children to Lisieux where they were watched by an aunt. The eldest sister, Pauline, made herself the religious educator of the house and their sister Mary became the "mother" running the household. They all had their hands full with many things at once, especially in attending to the needs and wants of little Therese.

This behavior of wants and needs could have continued for the rest of Therese's life if it had not been for a fateful night one Christmas Eve in 1886. Therese was fourteen years old and had an immediate conversion to Christ that transformed her life forever. From that time on she was filled with the love of God and her mission in life was to use her high spirits and energy to be in service to others. She sought to do for others instead of thinking of herself and began a new life of sacrifice and service. Her family was moved by her transformation. They had always been a family dedicated to God, and this testimony furthered their commitment to God and service to Him.

Pauline, the eldest sister made a decision to enter the Carmelite order of Nuns at Lisieux. Therese, who would miss her terribly, began to think about entering the order at some point in her life, when she was old enough. Soon after another sister made the same decision as Pauline and went to join her in the convent, causing Therese great longing to go as well. But waiting till she was grown was too unbearable and after a year had passed she pleaded with her father to be allowed to join as well. He willingly agreed that she could become a Carmelite as well, but the Carmelite authorities, as well as the Bishop of Bayeux, refused to hear of it because of her young age. As despairing as this was, Therese never gave up the hope that she might be allowed to join, no matter how young she might be.

On a French pilgrimage with her father to Rome a few months later, she seized upon an opportunity during a public audience with the Pope to request permission to become a Carmelite nun. Kneeling before Pope Leo XIII for a blessing, Therese broke the rule of silence on this very auspicious occasion and asked him, "in honor of your jubilee, allow me to enter Carmel at fifteen." Pope Leo was clearly impressed by the confidence of the young girl, but upheld the decision of the immediate superiors.

But at the end of 1888 the bishop finally gave his permission and Therese entered the Carmel at Lisieux, taking the name of Theresa of the Child Jesus. This journey of faith as a Carmelite nun was a special gift for Therese and she took to the duties of the convent with great joy of heart and spirit. One of the principle duties of a Carmelite nun is to pray for priests and she placed her whole being into praying for them constantly.

Therese was not in the best of health, but in spite of her frail physical being, she always seemed to be in great spirits, smiling as she attended to her duties in the kitchen. The Carmelite rule was very strict and austere, yet photographs taken by her sister within the cloister show Therese having a grand time. The pictures show Therese wearing a costume of Joan of Arc for the play held by the sisters.

Louis Martin's health was failing, and with his other daughters living at the convent, his daughter Celine stayed at home to care for him. In 1894 Louis died and the fourth Martin sister, Celine, was now able to join the cloister as well. Now all was well, Therese thought. All of her sisters were with her serving their Lord together, just as it should be, together at last.

All was not well, though, and eighteen months later, Therese had a huge health setback. She began to hemorrhage from her mouth as the result of contracting Tuberculosis. Therese had lived an exemplarily life as a Carmelite nun, in fact the sisters were quite taken by her "little ways," a simple way of approaching life in love and gratitude. She lived each day confident in God's all abiding love, believing simply that God loved her, she loved Him, and she was to love others because of His love. She wrote "What matters in life is not great deeds but great love." Her spiritual teaching was one of attending to everyone in a spirit of love and devotion. Her focus was one of childlike faith, open and honest about everything in life, doing the ordinary with extraordinary love.

Therese also saw the seasons as reflecting the seasons of God's love affair with us. The greatest testimony to the childlike heart of Therese was in her love of flowers. She saw herself as the "little flower of Jesus," who gave glory to God by just being her beautiful little self among all the other flowers in God's garden. The endearing "little flower" analogy became associated with Therese forever after.

Therese's "little ways" were shown in the menial tasks she attended to in the convent. She served in the refectory, the laundry room and in the sacristan by taking care of the altar and chapel. She was also quite gifted in writing plays for the sisters to bring them joy and entertainment. Most importantly she tried to show all the nuns in the community the same devoted love. It may have been no easy task for her to love everyone equally, as there were some that could be most difficult at times.

Her mundane tasks and life seems so routine and ordinary, but it was in the simple ways that her love for Christ shone clearly. Her "little way" was precise and direct but required great commitment and resolve.

Her ability to grasp the love of God in the ordinary steps of life attracted others to Therese's simple and devoted faith. She sincerely believed that she was able to accomplish all that she did because of God's enduring love for her. God was generous to her with his love and therefore she was able to generously love others in the same way. She firmly believed that at the end of her life she would stand before her God empty handed. She held fast to the idea that all was accomplished in complete union with God.

Isn't it a grand notion to believe that holiness is within the reach of "ordinary" people by simply living out our lives with the confidence of God's love? "Simply living" is exactly right, reaching others in "little ways" in kindness and with thoughtfulness. When we continue to strive for more "stuff" and want more than we need, we clutter up our homes and our hearts with chasing after things that really don't matter. The old adage of less is more is a great ideal for us to embrace in this age of consumerism, and I for one would like to learn from Therese's "little ways."

The "little flower" became very ill from her tuberculosis and even though she had hoped that someday she might serve as a missionary, her disease was very advanced. The last eighteen months of her life were filled with great spiritual trials and immense physical suffering. In June of 1897, Therese was moved to the infirmary where she subsequently died on September 30 of that year.

Therese is well loved by Catholics and Protestants alike, and Pope Pius XI beatified her in 1924, and canonized her in 1925. She was named the heavenly patroness of all foreign missions, and of all works for Russia.

We will remember Therese Martin for her transformed life through the power of our Savior Jesus Christ. She was a self-absorbed child who became a God-absorbed spiritual being when she encountered the power of the Holy Spirit. Her life is a testimony to the great love of God for His children and the grace He offers each of us if we choose to make Him Lord of our lives. May you find Him now, if you have not known Him, and perhaps you too can become a child of the "little way."

"The Flower" by St. Theresa

All the earth with snow is covered,
Everywhere the white frosts reign;
Winter and his gloomy courtiers
Hold their court on earth again.
But for you has bloomed the flower
Of the fields, Who comes to earth
From the fatherland of heaven,
Where eternal spring has birth,
Near the Rose of Christmas, Sister!
In the lowly grasses hide,
And be like the humble flowerets,
Of heaven's King the lowly bride!

Scripture Application

AT THAT TIME THE DISCIPLES CAME TO JESUS AND ASKED, "WHO IS THE GREATEST IN THE KINGDOM OF HEAVEN?" HE CALLED A LITTLE CHILD AND HAD HIM STAND AMONG THEM. AND HE SAID: "I TELL YOU THE TRUTH, UNLESS YOU CHANGE AND BECOME LIKE CHILDREN, YOU WILL NEVER ENTER THE KINGDOM OF HEAVEN. THEREFORE, WHOEVER HUMBLES HIMSELF LIKE THIS CHILD IS THE GREATEST IN THE KINGDOM OF HEAVEN.

MATTHEW 18:1-4

Reflections on Faith for "the Little Way":

Can you think of little ways you can show others your love for them and for God? What can you do to enjoy your daily work with joy and contentment?

Doesn't it sound like freedom to be able to live simply, focusing on God, family and friends? Work is important too, even when you don't care for what you do. What ways you can make the most menial tasks more enjoyable?

Dedicate the hardest job you have to do to Jesus, and give your all in whatever that might be. Whether it is scrubbing pots, mopping floors or designing sky scrapers, do everything in excellence for our heavenly Father.

Faith

of

Poets, Writers

and

Composers

Introduction to
Part Three

Faith of Poets, Writers and Composers

We all have favorite novelists, musicians, poets and artists and have marveled at the intrinsic way they seem to use words, melodies, cadence and mesmerizing visions to capture our imaginations. Where does this seemingly endless creativity spring from? When listening to Mozart, the Beatles or some favorite, moving hymn do you feel yourself being immersed in the music and lyrics? When reading Tolstoy, Twain or devouring an inspirational book, can you imagine yourself being lifted up and carried away by the words? On beholding paintings created by Renoir, Monet or Norman Rockwell, do you sometimes pause at the mastery and wonder of the work of art?

Our Creator, Almighty God, has imbued each and every one of us with gifts and talents that stretch imaginations into grand ideas and possibilities. Some are gifted in music and can sing or play an instrument, neither of which I can do. Others are gifted with their hands and can sculpt, paint, draw or design beautiful clothing and jewelry that would even make King Solomon gasp. This never-ending array of creativity in the world displays the essence of God the Father, Creator of the Universe. God has given these gifts graciously to mankind, and for those of us who serve Him it is our great pleasure to use these gifts in ways that bless others and magnify Him.

These treasures that break forth from His children are inspired because of the love that Jesus Christ has for them. To show Jesus how much we love Him through our obedient use of any gift He has given us is a true privilege. This is the ultimate in expression, giving creativity back to the Creator. This is our gift to Him, radiating His love back to Him through our measure of gifts and talent. This, then, is the God-breathed faith that inspires creativity.

CARDINAL FLOWER

THE CARDINAL FLOWER CANNOT BE MISSED IN THE GARDEN WITH ITS
RED PLUMES REGALLY ANNOUNCING TO THE WORLD ITS PURPOSE. IT
WILL NOT GO UNNOTICED BUT WILL ELECTRIFY SOULS THROUGHOUT THE
AGES, GLORIFYING GOD FOREVER. HILDEGARD VON BINGEN WAS SUCH A
FORCE DURING HER LIFETIME OF SERVICE TO OUR GOD.

Hildegard von Bingen

1098 – 1179

Visionary, Author and Composer

During the end of the eleventh century, in 1098, a daughter was born into a family in Bingen, Germany, and it was something of a joyous occasion. This child was the tenth to be born into the family, and was the daughter of a knight. Now the custom of the time dictated that the tenth child be dedicated to the church upon birth, not out of some profound religious obligation, but rather out of the necessity of being able to feed an extra child.

At the age of eight years, Hildegard traveled to a monastery at Mount St. Disibode to receive a religious education from an "anchoress" by the name of Jutta. Being an "anchor" of the church was even more difficult that becoming a nun and was indeed a high, religious career. Many young women entered into convent life during the medieval period and pursued a holy life, set apart from the world. When Hildegard was eighteen she became a nun, and by the time she was thirty-eight, she was named head of the all nuns at her monastery.

You may wonder, what is so unusual or special about Hildegard the nun? I honestly wondered too and then I began to research this fantastic woman of God and could hardly believe what I was reading. It was the blessed way in which God began to work in her that is astounding, and the only way to experience Hildegard is to embrace her totally.

Incredible visions would overtake this middle-aged nun, so intertwined in her being that she began to write them down in order to share them with others. Before she decided that they must be shared, she prayed thoughtfully and deliberated personally on whether others in her religious community could benefit from them. She entitled her visions the *Scivias* or "Know the Ways." It took her a total of ten years to put them in writing.

Soon Pope Eugenius III became aware of her writings and sent representatives to visit her and bring back a few samples of her writing. The pope found her writing very interesting, and he was so pleased that he gave Hildegard and her *Scivia* a blessing. It was because of the pope's blessing that news spread quickly throughout the church and many girls and women traveled to meet Hildegard. News seemed to travel at great speed in the early Catholic Church, and before too long the monastery, which also housed monks, became overcrowded. Hildegard decided that she needed to relocate and began to envision a new monastery just for women. This new monastery would be built on a mountainside in Rupersberg, and she was instrumental in both design and construction of the residence. This was no easy process, but it would boast of the first-mentioned use of metal pipes that would bring fresh, running water indoors.

While the women were getting settled in the newly constructed monastery, Hildegard restarted her religious study and writing. It was also at this time, between 1158 and 1170 that she began traveling through southern Germany, Paris and Switzerland. Traveling by horseback and often times by boat, she stopped at small churches and cathedrals and preached to the people of the villages. These messages proved so popular that people often requested copies.

But there were more than just visions and inspirational messages from Hildegard. Other gifts began to develop within her faithful heart. She began composing music, hauntingly beautiful, lifting both body and soul out and up towards the majesty of God. This gift, this incredibly inspiring talent, would be what would keep Hildegard's name alive through the ages.

Hildegard's plain chants or Gregorian chants number seventy-two and are often described as beautiful and ethereal. In the medieval era of male-dominated composers, her compositions stand out, and she is considered one of the most important women composers of all time. Just when I thought that this must be the limit of her gifts, I discovered that she wrote a play with musical accompaniment, nearly seventy poems, and nine books. Not to mention that two of her books were written about herbal medicine and the human body, and her other books contained writings about saints and theological texts. Hildegard was also a great writer of letters to a variety of people, including popes, bishops, kings and other leaders, some still in existence to this very day. But music was her true passion and calling in life. She wrote:

"Sometimes when we hear a song we breathe deeply and sigh. This reminds the prophet that the soul arises from heavenly harmony. In thinking about this, he was aware that the soul has something in itself of this music."

It is in reading some of her work that you can sense the inner purity and beauty that compelled her to write of her love of God.

"Listen, there was once a king sitting on his throne. Around him stood great and wonderfully beautiful columns ornamented with ivory, bearing the banners of the king with great honor. Then it pleased the king to raise a small feather from the ground, and he commanded it to fly. The feather flew, not because of anything in itself but because the air bore it along. Thus am I, a feather on the breath of God."

On September 17, 1179, Hildegard Von Bingen drew her last breath and died at the age of eighty-one. Throughout her life she lived true to her calling and gave her all for God, using her gifts to magnify the true character of our righteous God. She was an amazing woman who lived an amazing life, refusing to be restricted by the social norms of her day when women were not known for religious writings, preaching, or composing inspirational music.

Hildegard Von Bingen's music can still be heard some nine hundred years later on CDs, and her books have been translated into many languages. Her writings are collected in important religious texts, and her life and legacy are still with us today. Hildegard got to do what she absolutely loved and not only blessed the world during her lifetime but ours as well. To top it all off, she gets to be present with Jesus our Savior and with all the witnesses that have gone before us. What a blessed life indeed!

Scripture Application

> ... THE SIMPLICITY THAT IS IN
> CHRIST.
>
> 2 CORINTHIANS 11:3

Reflections on Faith for Discerning Your Calling:

Hildegard's Scripture verse speaks of the simplicity that is in Christ. Do you see how truly simple God's plan is for His children when we embrace Christ as our Savior? He leads us in using our gifts, and when we stay true to our natural calling, our service to Him remains simple.

Sometimes we run after other gifts or talents that are not our own, thinking surely our meager abilities can't be used for anything. What can you do to shift your perception about this type of thinking? What one or two things are you talented in? If you can't think of anything that you're good at, ask your best friend, your spouse, or a co-worker what they see as your talents. Most importantly, ask God. Then agree with God to embrace your gifts and use them for His glory, to magnify Him and bring others into the saving grace of Jesus Christ.

AFRICAN DAISY
THE HUMBLE AFRICAN DAISY SPEAKS GENTLENESS, LIKE OUR LORD. ITS
DELICATE, TINY FLOWERS GROUP TOGETHER AMID THE PROTECTION OF
SOFT BUT STRONG SURROUNDING LEAVES. THIS WAS PHILLIS WHEATLEY,
CONFIDENT, SURE AND DETERMINED TO MAKE THE BEST OF HER GOD-
GIVEN GIFTS AND TALENTS IN THE AGE IN WHICH SHE LIVED.

Phillis Wheatley

c. 1753 – 1784

African-American Poet

Knowing that each century has within its own political and societal schisms factors that determine success rates for women living within its confines, Phillis Wheatley rose above convention. The fact that Phillis possessed the ability to read and write during a time when most women were not highly educated was singularly significant, but because she was a slave it was profound.

Phillis Wheatley was born in Senegal, West Africa, around the year 1753 when she was kidnapped and brought to America on a slave ship in 1761. In Boston that same year she was sold at a slave auction to the family of John Wheatley, a prominent Boston merchant. The Wheatley family treated Phillis with love and respect, offering her the unusual privilege for a slave of learning to read and write. It became most obvious to the family that she had a remarkable intelligence, so she was made a charge of Mary Wheatley, who at fifteen was one of the most highly educated girls in Boston. Mary, who had an inquisitive nature and penchant for knowledge, enjoyed teaching Phillis to read and write. Nathaniel, Mary's twin brother, was also enlisted to tutor her charge in Latin.

The family made sure to teach Phillis the tenets of the Christian faith. The Bible became a well-spring to her and she came to know it quite well, becoming a Christian at a young age. When she was fourteen, she began to write poetry and had her first work published in 1767 entitled, "On Messrs. Hussey and Coffin," which appeared in the *Newport Mercury*. Another poem followed on the death of the Reverend George Whitefield, the great evangelical preacher who frequently toured New England, titled, *An Elegiac Poem on the Death of the Celebrated Divine, George Whitefield.* This poem was widely read in publications throughout the east, in Boston, Newport, and Philadelphia, giving Phillis instant recognition and becoming a sensation in Boston in the late 1770s.

Phillis' fame spread even further when her poems turned up in London and stirred the souls of England. Selena Hastings, Countess of Huntingdon, a good friend of Reverend Whitefield, was so taken by Phillis' poems, that she extended an invitation for her to visit her in London. With Selena's assistance Phillis had her first book of poems published in 1773, sending the whole of Britain to laud her as England's most acclaimed poet. Her reputation grew quickly with Selena Hasting's aid and Phillis soon became quite the celebrity across Europe, as well as in America.

This fame was rather short lived due to a crisis that arose in the Wheatley household. Phillis' beloved family was faced with the ill health of Mrs. Wheatley. In addition, with Mary expecting another child, Phillis decided to return home in 1773 to care for them. It seemed for awhile that Mrs. Wheatley was regaining her health while under Phillis' tender care, but she relapsed and died on March 3, 1774. The family was utterly devastated by her death. Within a short time John Wheatley died as well, leaving a mountain of debt that forced the sale of his home, leaving Phillis displaced but a free woman.

Phillis married John Peters, a free black man, in 1776. She looked forward to helping him to operate a grocery store that he had just opened. They had two children, a son, Johnny, who died as a young boy and a daughter by the name of Susan. Things did not go as well as Phillis had prayed, and when they threw John Peters into debtors' prison she had to try and make a living for her daughter and herself. This time around her poems did not seem to gather any interest and she was rejected everywhere she turned because of her race. After trying in vain to find a publisher she was forced to turn to a job as a scrub woman in a boarding house.

When her health began to deteriorate (she had suffered from asthma most of her life) Phillis struggled to continue working, and because of her faith she was strengthened when all else failed. Even being impoverished did not deter her from pursuing her writing and the dream that she might someday be published again. It was with great anguish that she soon realized that not only race fought against her, but the post revolutionary economy was creating a struggle for everyone. She was able to publish a few of her poems in 1784 under the name of Phillis Peters, but she would never see the earlier acclaim that had graced her life. Her creativity still lived brightly in her spirit, but her physical health was never the same. On December 5, 1784, she died in abject poverty.

Phillis Wheatley was blessed with a literary genius that allowed her to move above circumstances that would have kept most people in creative bondage. She grew in her faith, uplifted in her belief in Jesus Christ, and stepped out of the box to celebrate her giftedness in poetry. Her ability to recognize God's gifts and her determination to utilize them shined through her perseverance in embracing opportunity.

Scripture Application

"DID NOT OUR HEARTS BURN WITHIN US?"

LUKE 24:23

Reflections on Faith for Opportunity:

Have you been able to use your giftedness in unique ways to minister the Gospel of Jesus Christ to others?

When the doors of opportunity open do you walk in with confidence, or do you hesitate to move?

Have you been able to discern when God was speaking to you about new opportunities? How does one develop that discernment in listening to God?

One way is to become quiet before the Lord, pray and listen with your heart. Journaling is another. Let everyone know your desire to share your gifts and talents and be available for whatever the Lord might have for you. Never give up on yourself. Believe in the One who has gifted you and loves you. He will use you to complete the work He has at hand.

BLEEDING HEART

Can you see that the Bleeding Heart flower stands as a symbol of love, a pledge of honor and integrity? Sarah Josepha Hale continued her pledge for justice and truth in all areas of life until the day that she died. Hers was a heart that willingly bled for mankind.

Sarah Josepha Hale

1788 – 1879

Author and Magazine Editor

It is comforting to know that women have always known in their heart of hearts that God intended for us to be treated with respect and dignity. Those women champions who have gone before us to pave the way that we may have the opportunities for higher education should be celebrated and recognized. In understanding the social constraints of each woman's individual era we can appreciate the great undertaking they endured to press forward for our rights. We should never take for granted the immense struggle these champions fought for our benefit. Because of their faithful determination that women everywhere should have basic rights we remain forever grateful and humbled. Here we celebrate one who gave her life for the betterment of ours, who blazed a straighter path for all our journeys.

On October 24, 1788, Sarah Beull was born in Newport, New Hampshire, to Captain Gordon Beull and Martha Whittlesay. Captain Beull had served in the Revolutionary War and displayed a grand example of patriotism that little Sarah readily embraced. Her mother was in charge of her education at home, and when her older brother Horatio became a student at Dartsmouth College he tutored his sister in all his classes. Horatio was responsible for Sarah's "higher education," and she thoroughly enjoyed learning subjects such as Latin and philosophy under his patient tutelage. This advanced manner of study allowed Sarah the opportunity to eventually open a school for boys and girls. It is reportedly at this school that she had an incident that became the basis for a poem that she wrote in 1830 as "Mary's Lamb" and later published as the much beloved "Mary Had a Little Lamb."

Sarah enjoyed her time of teaching, but soon a romance sprang up between her and the charming David Hale, a lawyer, and the decision to leave teaching to marry was an easy one. David and Sarah were married in 1813 at the Rising Star Tavern (which was also an inn) that her father owned after leaving his four hundred acre farm in Newport, New Hampshire. It was in this sleepy little New England town that David Hale established a law practice. Theirs was an easy, loving relationship, sharing much in common, often sitting by the glow of the fire in their home enjoying interests such as botany, a very popular study in Victorian times, as well as geology, mineralogy and French. They were so keenly into their pursuit of intellectual study, that they set aside two hours every evening from 8 P.M. to 10 P.M. for this sole purpose.

But circumstances have an uneasy way of disrupting a promising life of married bliss, and for Sarah and David trouble was coming. An unforeseen snowstorm in September caught David Hale by surprise as he travelled home in a horse and carriage from the adjoining town of Guild. Regrettably he never recovered from the pneumonia that settled into his lungs from the exacerbating effect of being caught in the cold for so long a time. David Hale died on September 25, 1822, and his wife Sarah became a widow at the young age of thirty-five.

Sarah and David had been delighted to bring four children into the world together and at the time of his death she was pregnant with their fifth child. Two weeks after his passing Sarah went into labor and on October 9, 1822, she gave birth to her second son, William George. He joined his sisters, Frances Ann, three, Sarah Josepha, two, and oldest son David Emerson, seven.

Being widowed with five children all under the age of seven is no easy task for anyone, but especially so for a woman in the 19th century. Being an excellent seamstress, Sarah decided that one way she could earn a living to support her family was to sew for other people. With the financial backing of the Freemasons, who had been friends of her husband, Sarah was able to open a millinery shop in town with her sister-in-law.

The work was not much to Sarah's liking, nor very enjoyable so she spent every spare moment engaged in reading or writing. Having been an avid reader for most of her life it was a natural progression for her to write about the things that she was passionate about. Upon penning a book of poetry entitled, *The Genius of Oblivion and Other Original Poems*, her husband's friends financed its publication in 1823. The success of this first effort proved just fruitful enough to allow her the time to leave the millinery shop and pursue the writing of a novel. *Northwood: A Tale of New England* was set in the midst of the growing tension between the north and south concerning the issue of slavery. This backdrop provided Sarah with a platform to challenge America in its struggle against the inhumane practice of "owning" fellow human beings for financial gain. This novel was published in 1827 and catapulted Sarah Hale's name into America's consciousness.

The book sold very well and is considered by many to be the first important American novel written by a woman. This stirring book undoubtedly opened a future door for an even more well-known writer by the name of Harriet Beecher Stowe and her life-altering novel *Uncle Tom's Cabin*. President Abraham Lincoln, upon meeting Harriet Beecher Stowe, said to her, "So you're the little lady who started this war." No doubt Lincoln had read Sarah Hale's book first, realizing the impact she had on the American people early on in the struggle for freeing the slaves. Her ultimate mission in life would bless Americans for generations to come.

When *Northwood* came out in 1827, it brought Mrs. Hale to the attention of Reverend John Blake of Boston who was looking to launch a new publication for women that same year. Reverend Blake invited Sarah to consider becoming the editor of the magazine, a position that would give her the voice that would nurture women with domesticity and social influence. Taking two of her youngest children with her to Boston she embraced the offer with gratitude and cheer, buoyed by the possibilities of the enterprise at hand. *Ladies Magazine* began with modest expectations, growing first with a name change of *American Ladies Magazine* to a complete change when in 1830 it was purchased by Louis Godey of Philadelphia. It would become known as *Godey's Lady's Book* and that is where Sarah Josepha Hale hit her highest point as an editor in the world of women's magazines.

Sarah liked to be called the "editress," not editor of the journal, rather enjoying the more feminine title over the formal male title. "The Book" was a much anticipated edition in women's lives of the time, as there was much content for intellectual hunger, but at the same time satisfying recipes, household tips, child-rearing, and the allure of all the latest fashions. It is noted with some irony that as progressive as Mrs. Hale seemed to be, she had little regard for the trends in fashion and intimated to the owner of *Godey's Lady's Book* that the women would be better served if they left out all the color plates of costumes that were featured regularly. Greatly resenting their inclusion, she reluctantly included them out of deference to Mr. Godey.

Mrs. Hale was born into a society of great social constraints, the Victorian Era, full of impositions on women to consistently behave in a most dignified and restrained manner. Much was forbidden to them. And girls were raised with the understanding that their lives were not their own, but that they were bound to their parents until married and then were little more than property to their husbands. Limited or no education was offered and the thought of women in the workplace was practically unheard of unless they were maids, or some other subservient domestic worker. Women of a higher station were not allowed to do such work, and if one happened to be unfortunate enough to have lost their well-being, they were lost to friends and family in their bid to eke out a meager living. No one would want to associate with them if they were leveled to an impoverished, washer woman state of being. Without a husband, a woman could disappear into servitude. Without friends or family to offer financial help of some kind a woman was destined to become destitute and alone in the world.

Sarah Hale brought hope and a transition of sorts for women to come out of this era of bondage into a new way of thinking. This transition from the eighteenth century's consideration of women as highly prized chattel into the nineteenth century's dream of women actually achieving economic and moral freedom would be her legacy.

Sarah proved worthy of the task at hand and as chief editor her features in the magazine broke new ground. It was her decision to include the works of American women authors instead of the popular European male writers of the day that shook things up in the women's magazine genre. Even though Sarah was progressive in her views of women in the area of education, she staunchly advocated that a woman's place was in the home. This seems to be a conflict of interest, but she was after all a Christian woman in the Victorian era. Her strong convictions included the belief that women should not be allowed to vote, probably due to her dislike of the Suffragettes' militant attitudes. Her notion of women's advancement was more in line with gaining educational ground and respect as a human being.

As a Victorian woman Sarah was not quite ready to throw away the ideals of women being good wives, mothers and purveyors of domestic tranquility. It was very clear in her magazine that she believed that women should be encouraged in the elevation of their role as homemakers. In fact she always referred to homemaking as "domestic science" and used this image in her housekeeping guides and cookbooks. It was through the home that she believed women could best inspire men to accomplish greater things for their private and public lives. She actually believed that women were superior to men, and prescribed to the idea that God designed creation in a lower to higher order. So from amoeba to man, and ultimately to woman, he had designed a natural progressive order of intelligence, resulting in woman. Therefore women, she believed, should embrace their calling to hearth and home and advance man's efforts in the world. An interesting concept!

She championed women's colleges and urged that women not only be allowed to attend them but to teach in them. When Elizabeth Blackwell's determination to pursue an education as a physician caused public outcry, Sarah supported her cause. She believed that single women should be trained in medical skills and allowed to do the work of a missionary. This argument fueled her passion to support missions, and she served as an officer in the Women's Union Missionary Society and the Ladies' Medical Missionary Society.

It was Sarah's dedication to women's education that resulted in her advocacy for an all women's college, suggesting to her friend Michael Vassar that the teachers hired should be all women. When Vassar College opened there were twenty-two women and only eight male faculty. Through the magazine Sarah was able to give the new school an incredible amount of support and advance publicity. Her endorsements in her editorials generated great interest among women, and her personal opinion helped spur enrollments. The only criticism she had for the college was the name that was chosen: Vassar's Female College. She was fairly repulsed at the categorical species label of "female" and urged students to cross out female and write in "girl" or "woman" whenever they came across the term in print.

Sarah remained a prolific writer. One important book she wrote was *Woman's Record; or, Sketches of All Distinguished Women from the Creation to A.D.1854, Arranged in Four Eras, with Selections from Female Writers of Every Age.* This long-winded title went through three editions, and even to the modern reader it is amusing evidence of Sarah's personality. Sarah included many diverse women of history, including those who were malevolent. She never outwardly condemned controversial figures, but rather gave the facts leaning toward trying to understand the ill-behaved person with a forgiving slant of view. On Catherine the Great, Empress of Russia, she wrote: "Whatever her own irregularities, she strictly discountenanced violations of decorum."

Sarah's position as editor of such a prestigious magazine enabled her to champion important causes. She rallied support for the Bunker Hill battle monument, the preservation of Mount Vernon, and the greatest campaign of her lifetime, the establishment of a National Day of Prayer.

Sarah's deep Christian values coursed strongly through her veins, and one of her greatest desires was to have a National Day of Prayer for America. There had previously existed officially proclaimed days of thanksgiving, but she believed that the American people needed a national holiday, celebrating our country's gratitude to Almighty God. The Puritans were the first to set aside a day of thanksgiving and they actually fasted, rather than feasted. The same was true when George Washington designated a day of collective thanksgiving, praying and fasting to show God the nation's gratitude. The Continental Congress set aside December 18 as a Day of Thanksgiving and Praise to be observed by all the colonies.

Sarah Josepha Hale felt compelled to write to President Abraham Lincoln and compel him to make the annual thanksgiving "a national and fixed Union Festival." During this time she had built the readership of *Godey's Lady's Book* to 150,000, and her editorials on the subject could not easily be ignored. Her annual Thanksgiving editorial in her magazine began with Nehemiah 8:10: "Then he said unto them, 'Go your way, eat the fat, and drink the sweet, and send portions unto them for whom nothing is prepared; for this day is holy unto our Lord; neither be ye sorry; for the joy of the Lord is your strength.'"

It was Sarah's strong Episcopal faith that fueled her argument that if Nehemiah set aside a time of thanksgiving in a time of national stress, "in a time of national darkness and sore troubles, shall we not recognize the goodness of God never faileth, and that to our Father in Heaven we should always bring the Thanksgiving offering at the ingathering of the harvest?"

Sarah's other passion was the continued plight of the slaves. With the Civil War raging she fell upon the idea that would fuel freedom for those in bondage and solidify a nation in a Day of Thanksgiving. With her abolitionist sentiments woven throughout her text, she suggested to her readers that if 40,000 churches would accept donations on a Day of Thanksgiving they could use the funds to free the slaves so that all of America could truly be free. This was not just literary page filler, it was what she really wanted churches to do, raise money to set the slaves free.

In fact she began an enthusiastic letter writing campaign with the help of her assistant to accomplish her goal. They sent out thousands of handwritten letters to lobby politicians for a national holiday. Amazingly this very direct way of reaching the masses resulted in success. The letters and her newspaper editorials touched the hearts of politicians and citizens alike rallying them to unite for a Day of Thanksgiving under the official designation from Lincoln.

The timing of Sarah's push for a national day of prayer coincided with the President's desire to promote national unity. He ordered Seward to draft the proclamation. On October 3, in the early morning hours, Lincoln read the proclamation:

The year that is drawing toward its close has been filled with the blessings of fruitful fields and helpful skies. To these bounties, which are so constantly enjoyed that we are prone to forget the source from which they come, others have been added, which are of so extraordinary a nature that cannot fail to penetrate and soften the heart which is habitually insensible to the ever watchful providence of Almighty God.

Secretary of State William H. Seward wrote, "No human counsel hath devised, nor hath any mortal hand worked out these great things. They are the gracious gift of the Most High God, who, while dealing with us in anger for our sins, hath nevertheless remembered mercy."

President Lincoln moved forward with an annual Day of Thanksgiving that would be observed on the last Thursday in November. [This day would change a couple of times.] At the beginning of this official proclamation Lincoln stirs our hearts with these words:

> It is the duty of nations as well as of men to own their dependence upon the overruling power of God; to confess their sins and transgressions in humble sorrow, yet with assured hope that genuine repentance will lead to mercy and pardon; and to recognize the sublime truth, announced in the Holy Scriptures and proven by all history, that those nations only are blessed whose God is the Lord.

Profound words by a profound President, calling a nation's people to humble themselves before God for forgiveness and mercy.

Sarah basked in gratitude for the hard won battle that she had fought, mostly through her succession of editorials and letter writing. This was Sarah's greatest achievement and it was a hard won process that took over fifteen dedicated years to achieve. Using her popular magazine as a platform to promote her dream for a national Day of Thanksgiving for the United States she realized her goal. She brought a nation that had been torn apart by a savage war, a conflict that pitted brother against brother, and drove it humbly to its knees.

Sarah had been a demure, young, Victorian woman, who when married supposed she would fulfill her calling by tending to hearth and home. A beautiful woman with trademark long curls and expressive eyes, she unpredictably had become her nation's inspiration in their darkest hour. Her New England heritage speaks of her hearty, Yankee stock that when pressed upon with the challenges of life, marched on in stalwart perseverance.

Sarah Joseph Buell Hale retired at the age of ninety, writing: "I must bid farewell to my countrywomen, with the hope that this work of half a century may be blessed to the furtherance of their happiness and usefulness in their divinely-appointed sphere." She died the next year at the age of ninety-one and left behind a grateful nation.

Scripture Application

ENTER HIS GATES WITH
THANKSGIVING AND HIS
COURTS WITH PRAISE;
GIVE THANKS TO HIM
AND PRAISE HIS NAME.

PSALM 100:4

Reflections on Faith for Determination:

When facing a particularly difficult time in life, are you able to focus on the solution and not the problem? Are you overwhelmed with stressors in life, without being able to see a way out of them? Could you be as creative as Sarah was in her resolve to find a means to earn a living?

What kinds of work do you find creative and inspiring? Become determined to find out.

What Scriptures can help keep you encouraged and enthusiastic about life? One way is to use your concordance to look up Scriptures that pertain to perseverance and steadfastness. Now that's faith in action.

"MANY HEARTS" FLOWER

THE "MANY HEARTS" FLOWER IS ALSO CALLED ST. SIMEON'S FLOWER
(SEE LUKE 2:35). THIS SWEET FLOWER CALLS TO THE HEART, SOFTLY
PROCLAIMING GOD'S LOVE. CHARLOTTE ELLIOTT SUFFERED IN BOTH
MIND AND BODY, BUT SURRENDERED HER ALL TO THE SAVIOR AND
FOUND PEACE AND REST.

Charlotte Elliott

1789 – 1871

Hymn Writer

I t is always amazing when we see people who are able to attend to their lives when they are in the throes of pain and exhaustion. We know the Apostle Paul suffered with an affliction that so tormented him that he prayed three times for God to remove it and accepted the fact that in his life healing was not going to happen. How did Paul resolve to move forward in all he was called to do in the midst of his personal suffering? He claimed that through the power and strength of Christ he was able to be satisfied with whatever his circumstances might be. To suffer in affliction and still maintain creativity, love for God and your fellowman in this world is a tremendous testimony of the Glory of Christ. Charlotte Elliott was just one such person.

Though physical suffering plagued Charlotte Elliott for most of her life, her faith in God was a resounding testimony for all who knew her. Born in Clapham, England, in 1789, she was the daughter of Charles Elliott and granddaughter of Reverend Henry Venn, an eminent leader in the Church of England. Brought up amid refined, cultured Christians, Charlotte was such a happy girl that she earned the nickname of "Carefree Charlotte." Unusually well educated, she gravitated toward the arts and music, becoming a gifted portrait artist. With this skill she was able to earn her living as a young woman in her chosen profession while also displaying a gift as a writer of humorous verse.

Charlotte's first thirty years were filled with much joy and blessings, but shortly after her thirtieth birthday her health took a dramatic turn for the worse. It was a sudden malady, rendering her incapacitated physically, mentally and certainly spiritually. Charlotte described her condition as, "frequent bodily feelings of overpowering weakness, exhaustion day after day, hour after hour and great physical suffering." She was forced to spend her days in bed, unable to participate in the work she loved or enjoy the people in her once active life. This maelstrom brought much pain with no end in sight, leaving the once carefree Charlotte depressed and despondent, accusing God of her suffering. This debilitating illness lingered on for years and the besieged artist could hardly continue to survive in this poor condition.

Charlotte's father, who was a devout Christian, invited his friend Dr. Cesar Malan, a Swiss minister, evangelist and musician, to their home for dinner. It was through her father's prayerful invitation that he hoped Dr. Malan might be able to bring some much needed cheer to his deeply distressed daughter. At the end of dinner Dr. Malan leaned forward and commented to Charlotte that he hoped she was a Christian, to which she replied curtly, "I would rather not discuss that question." Malan apologized if there had been any offense.

This seemingly minor exchange would have a profound effect on Charlotte who could not shake Dr. Malan's comment from her head. His words had been a witness and proved to be a turning point in her pain-ridden, angry life. When she met the kind doctor again some three weeks later she told him about her being unable to forget what he had said to her and had been trying to find Jesus, her Savior. She struggled with understanding how she could come to Him. "You have nothing of merit to bring to God. You must come just as you are," replied the minister. Rejoicing, Charlotte did.

Dr. Malan's challenge to her to bring her fears, bitterness and resentment to the Lamb of God who takes away the sins of the world had convicted her and she put her trust in Jesus. Each year thereafter Charlotte would celebrate her "spiritual birthday" remembering and rejoicing in the day she went from despair to faith. Instead of the constant hate and anger that had consumed her she embraced the peace and joy that Dr. Malan had spoke of in his plea to come "just as you are."

The crippling infirmity that plagued her could not dampen her spiritual growth or her glowing love for her Savior Jesus. She wanted to be useful in life, even though she was restricted in her physical being. One of her contributions was to edit the *Religious Remembrancer* magazine and when her brother was raising funds for the daughters of clergymen-St. Mary's Hall, she asked to help. With her heart in the right place it was hard to realize that she was unable to be of assistance to her brother because of her illness. Feeling terribly inadequate and useless she fell into deep doubt and struggled with what she should do. As she thought about her situation it occurred to her that perhaps she could write a song for others who were in a similar situation. The inspired words she wrote became one of the greatest soul-winning songs in the history of hymns:

> *Just as I am, without one plea,*
> *But that Thy blood was shed for me*
> *And that Thou bidd'st me come to Thee*
> *O' Lamb of God, I come! I come!*

Many, many lives have been changed by the verses that Charlotte penned in her moments of despair and doubt. The transformation stories related to this hymn are known far and wide. In fact Dora Wordsworth, daughter of William Wordsworth, asked to have the lines read to her again and again on her death bed. An official in British-controlled India, Sir Henry Norman, was saved through the hymn at a meeting led by Lord Radstock. How many of us have heard the plaintive notes of this invitational call, "Just as I Am," at the end of a Billy Graham Crusade?

Copies of the song's verses were eventually sold to provide funds for the very school for poor clergyman that her brother had been raising funds for in 1836. Charlotte was still living when this transpired and realized that God had used her after all to bless this long ago project. "Just as I Am" became Charlotte's "spiritual autobiography," as she often referred to it, and just as it changed her life, it changed others' lives as well. Some would say that God did not heal her physically, but the truth is she was healed spiritually, which was the ultimate triumph in her life.

Because of her deep suffering, Charlotte lovingly wrote her *Invalid's Hymn Book*, which was published in various editions from 1834 to 1854, and contained all together one hundred and fifteen of her hymns. There were many other poetic volumes by her containing such hymns as "Hours of Sorrow," 1836; "Hymns for a Week," 1839; and "Thoughts in Verse on Sacred

Subjects," 1869. According to *Julian's Dictionary* her hymns number about one hundred and fifty with a large percentage in common use. "Her verse is characterized by tenderness of feeling, plaintive simplicity, deep devotion, and perfect rhythm. For those in sickness and sorrow she has sung as few others have done." There is mutual agreement that Charlotte Elliott is one of the most popular hymnists that came out of the nineteenth century.

In spite of her immense suffering she was able to give the world inspiration through her hymns that were born out of gratefulness. The mercy and grace that she received from God through her acceptance of Christ was poured out in her hymns with a tenderness and sweetness of spirit. This could only come from faith born out of the humbleness of embracing God's will for her life.

Charlotte was not fond of publicity due to her infirm condition and preferred to remain confined to her home. Nearly all her books were published anonymously in the beginning with few knowing of her giftedness. Her identity became more widely known as the public longed to know of the hymnist behind the life-changing lyrics. For more than fifty years Charlotte endured tremendous pain until her death on September 22, 1871, when she was eighty-three years of age. Upon her death more than a thousand letters were found among her papers, written by people whose lives had been touched by her hymn, "Just as I Am."

Charlotte Elliott overcame suffering and pain to touch people who may have been comfortless had she not used her gift to bring light and life to the lost.

Scripture Application

> I NOW REJOICE IN MY
> SUFFERINGS FOR YOU,
> AND FILL UP IN MY FLESH
> WHAT IS LACKING IN THE
> AFFLICTIONS OF CHRIST,
> FOR THE SAKE OF HIS
> BODY, WHICH IS THE
> CHURCH.
>
> COLOSSIANS 1:24

Reflections on Faith During Suffering

Are you in pain? Do you wake each day and wonder how you can possibly face another moment on this earth? Do you know others that suffer with affliction?

Mental distress, emotional hurts, addictions, and physical pain can crush our resolve to live for Christ into an ashen heap of nothingness.

Come today determined to live only in the moment, just as you are. For this moment is all we truly have to live for Him. Give our Lord Jesus your entire being and do not hold back but surrender yourself totally that He may lift you up and out of your pit.

OBEDIENT FLOWER
ONE NOTICES IMMEDIATELY THE LOVELY ARRAY OF PURPLE FLOWERS
CASCADING AGAINST THE GREEN LEAVES OF THE OBEDIENT FLOWER.
HANNAH MORE WAS JUST LIKE THIS FLOWER, SEEMINGLY ON DISPLAY TO
REPOSE IN THE GARDEN, BUT OBEDIENTLY REACHING TO NEW HEIGHTS
IN HER EFFORTS TO HELP THE LESS FORTUNATE OF THE WORLD.

Hannah More

1745 – 1833

Evangelical Writer and Abolitionist

The movie *Amazing Grace* brought the parliamentary leader William Wilberforce to the forefront of people's knowledge concerning his fight to end slavery in England. To know he was a mentor and encourager of a woman writer and evangelist is both thrilling and inspiring. This passionate believer in Christ was an encourager of Hannah More, who had a profound influence on the society she lived in.

Miss More was the most influential female philanthropist of her day according to Patricia Demmer (1996). And Anne Stott (2003) has described her as the "first Victorian." Her activities, theories, and practices as an educator and her involvement in pressure group politics are certainly worth noting. It was her passionate belief in liberty and freedom for the poor and disenfranchised that has left it's most indelible mark on history. Her literary ability in the realm of Christian literature for students was instrumental in the development of Sunday schools. Hannah became involved with her sister Martha in this approach to youth education and developed religious tracts for "informal" education. Modern day writers like Young and Ashton (1956) and Milson (1979) echo this sentiment in their support of Miss More's contribution as a central figure in the formation of youth work.

Jacob More, Hannah's father was the headmaster of a foundation school in Stapleton (Fishponds) near Bristol where she was born in 1745. All of the five More girls possessed strong, unique personalities, but Hannah, who was the fourth born, was delicate and high strung. She was easily stimulated and was oversensitive to criticism but could be very affectionate. The girls were brought up by their father to become teachers, starting their training at an early age. He was rather ambivalent about education for girls, feeling that too much book learning could cause irreparable harm to the female brain. Jacob was alarmed at his daughter Hannah's quick intelligence and wasn't sure what to make of her.

With all of the girl's exhibiting an independent streak, Jacob was certain his daughters would do well in life. When the three oldest sisters decided to open a boarding school for young ladies he gave them his blessing. Being very young, only nineteen, seventeen and fourteen at the start of their venture, it was interesting to their father to see the knack they had at making and developing important contacts. The school initially developed startup capital through funds raised by subscription, thus becoming a success from the very start.

The friendships they acquired were significantly diverse and socially important to the young ladies as they established the school in 1785 at 6 Trinity Street, College Green, Bristol. The range of people their activities attracted were such notables as Charles and John Wesley, who became friendly with Hannah's older sister Mary; James Ferguson, the astronomer; and Thomas Sheridan (the father of the playwright) lectured at the school. The younger sisters, Hannah and Martha, soon joined as part of the staff within a short time.

As Hannah grew into a young woman she attracted a suitor by the name of Edward Turner and soon became engaged. She was a lively enough girl with a quick wit and charming demeanor to the outside world. But it was her peculiar behavior in withdrawing from others in periods of depression and minor illnesses that gave her fiancé pause in going through with the marriage. With her many headaches, colds, and other functional illnesses, not to mention her ongoing depression, Edward kept postponing the wedding while worrying about Hannah's "indifferent temper." Eventually he was able to settle the manner by offering Miss More an annuity of £200 per year in order to become extricated from the engagement. To recover from his spurning, Hannah went to Uphill, near Weston-super-Mare under the guise of recuperation from a fever.

It has been said that because of her distressful broken engagement she resolved never to marry and began calling herself "Mrs. More." With this settled she set about to become a "woman of letters" (the annuity gave her the monetary help to accomplish this). Hannah had always had a penchant for writing poetry and had even written a play for her sister's school. With her literary skills she later decided to write for the stage and produced a professional play, *The Inflexible Captive* (later known as *Regulus*) that opened in 1775 at the Theatre Royal in Bath.

As an up and coming playwright, Hannah began visiting London in a series of annual events accompanied by two of her sisters, often taking lodging on Henrietta Street, Covent Garden. Sir Joshua Reynolds and his sister Frances (who was also a portrait painter) introduced London to Mrs. More and her sisters. Friendships were also developed with other theatrical and literary figures, and Hannah enjoyed engaging in a variety of activities with her new peers. This crowd was also known as the "blue stocking" circle. Through this clique the ingénue playwright was invited to stay with David Garrick and his wife Eva at their home in the Adelphi. There were many new plays that she wrote, and after David Garrick's death in 1779 Hannah stayed with Eva in the Adelphi house and took part in the conversation parties of the "blue stocking" circle.

Soon after this Hannah began to lose interest in the theater and the social scene that seemed to characterize London. She was disillusioned with effortless, meandering lifestyles and the relationships she had made through the "Blue stocking" circle. So she took to rewriting Bible stories in dialogue form. The deaths of her father, David Garrick, and other members of her London circle caused her great sadness and grief, making her more susceptible to the influence of the evangelical men and women of the Clapham Sect and other progressive religious groups. This particular sect was an informal, but influential group of wealthy evangelicals who sought to reinvigorate the Church of England. Their ideals were described as a modified form of Methodism and their auspicious members included Henry Venn (1725-97), William Wilberforce (1759-1833) and Zachary Macaulay (1768-1838), father of the historian Thomas Macaulay.

This most impressive contingency of men was strongly opposed to slavery and committed to missionary work. Additionally the Clapham Sect (so named because many of the members lived close to Clapham and worshipped in the parish church) was also involved in the foundation of the British and Foreign Bible Society in 1804.

It was Hannah More's good blessing and the hand of divine providence that brought her under the significant influence of William Wilberforce. Upon their meeting in 1786 in Bath he became a regular visitor to her new cottage at Cowslip Green and later to her house about a mile away at Barley Wood, where Hannah's sisters had joined her. It was William Wilberforce's fight against slavery and her own that sparked righteous indignation in the empathetic Hannah. Putting pen to paper she eloquently devised a poem entitled *Slavery* which when published in 1788 helped create an outcry of protest. This poem stands to this day as a witness to history's shame of the inequality and inhumanity of the slave trade.

There was a village by the name of Cheddar that had caught the ongoing attention of Wilberforce and on one of his visits he announced that "something had to be done for Cheddar." The condition of the people there troubled him greatly and after spending some time in the village he came away resolved that action must be taken to relieve both their physical as well as their spiritual discomforts. The fact that the people of Cheddar lacked spiritual comfort upset him grievously. An idea was formed out of their discussions that perhaps what was needed as a first step was a Sunday school. It was Hannah and Martha that opened such a school in Cheddar and within ten years they had set up more than a dozen Sunday schools.

The sisters agreed wholeheartedly that the poor of Cheddar must learn the structure of society in order to learn Christian principles. "Beautiful is the order of society," Hannah wrote, "when each according to his place, pays willing honor to his superiors—when servants are prompt to obey their masters, and masters deal kindly with their servants." In this we can see that obligation went both ways. Duties were reciprocal.

Hannah's "plan for instructing the poor" was "very limited and strict." Hannah wrote, "My object is not to teach dogmas and opinions, but to form the lower classes to habits of industry and virtue." The structure for this plan was clear. "I know no way of teaching morals," Hannah wrote, "but by teaching principles, nor of inculcating Christian principles without a good knowledge of Scripture."

As the Sunday school continued to thrive, Hannah More's activities and views came under the scrutiny of the Church of England. The evangelical wing approved of Sunday schools and similar ventures as a way forward and the more conservative wing viewed such "Methodist" activities as dangerous. This focus created a struggle within the church known as the "Blagdon Controversy" with the initial flame ignited at a Monday night meeting for adults that had been established by Hannah and Martha More. This meeting time was in essence a prayer gathering where people gave their testimonies.

The ongoing displeasure of the conservative leaders of the church grew heated and Hannah More was accused of being Methodistic. The local curate was deeply critical and the situation became the subject of various letters to the press with more than twenty pamphlets being distributed over a four year period. This debate only raged on in temper and accusations with Hannah being represented as a founder of a sect. With her physical health always precarious anyway, this round of insinuations and allegations only served to push her declining health over the edge and she collapsed. Hannah had to close Blagdon school and "she retreated from the world, believing that God had sent her poor health to turn her toward Him."

It was Hannah's view that the poor could learn to be physically comfortable as she showed them how to make better use of what they had, and as God molded them to be "submissive by teaching them that joy in Heaven was the recompense for deprivation on earth." Pressing forward as her health returned she wrote her first tract: *Village Politics, by Will Chip, a Country Carpenter.* The basic summary for the tract gave four arguments that "the gentry look after the worthy poor; no relation exists between government and want; government is no concern of the common man; God knows what is best for his people."

Quite impressively "Village Politics" sold numerous amounts of tracts, and More and other members of the Clapham group were encouraged to produce the "Cheap Repository Tracts." These tracts were a series of readable moral tales, prayers, sermons, uplifting ballads and a collection of readings. Hannah More wrote and edited many of the tracts, while others in their group raised money for printing and distribution. The first was published in March 1795 and the last was made some three years later. They were published monthly and overall sold in the millions with over one hundred produced, fifty of them by More. Hannah also wrote a number of books, one of which sold more than 30,000 copies in the United States before her death.

There has been much debate over Hannah More's views on women and their role in society. She seems to support the idea of education for women, but it is her reasons for women becoming educated that cloud the issue for most modern thinkers. It was her belief that women should be allowed an education instead of being forbidden to learn and then to scorn them for not knowing anything. She held that all women should be prepared for life rather than treated as an adornment, and that only exceptional girls receive the classical education that she and her sisters enjoyed. The average girl should be trained in whatever "inculcates principles, polishes taste, regulates temper, subdues passion, directs the feelings, habituates to reflections, trains to self-denial, and more especially, that which refers to all actions, feelings and tastes, and passions to the love and fear of God." She would have history taught to show the wickedness of mankind and guiding hand of God, and geography to indicate how Providence has graciously consulted man's comfort in suiting vegetation and climate to his needs.

Before we become too judgmental on dear Hannah, we must remember that she was living in the 18th century and the customs and social dictates were so far removed from where we are today. I can only applaud her for promoting the idea that girls receive some form of education at a time when women were not given the credit for the brains God gave them. Imagine how shocked she would be to see how far we women have come? I suppose, given her social framework, she would be both happy and appalled.

The Sunday school movement would be the driving force behind Hannah More's actions, and she continued the effort for the rest of her life. The fact that the villages they established schools in had so very little appalled her, so it was no surprise that William Wilberforce and the More sisters saw Sunday schooling as a way forward. At Cheddar in 1791, Hannah wrote:

> "We found more than 2,000 people in the parish, almost all very poor—no gentry, a dozen wealthy farmers, board, brutal and ignorant.... We went to every house in the place, and found every house a scene of the greatest vice and ignorance. We saw but one Bible in all the parish and that was used to prop a flower pot. No clergyman had resided in it for forty years. One rode

over from wells to preach once each Sunday. No sick were visited, and children were often buried without any funeral service."

Even more so appalling to Wilberforce and More was the fact that this situation had been apparently accepted by local worthies. The most significant factor Hannah believed, and possibly even the key, was the lack of religious knowledge among the poor and the lack of moral teaching.

The focus of teaching included instructing women, especially mothers to read, knit, and sew during weekday evenings. Hannah made a commitment to holding primary instruction on Sundays when people would be available from their work (hence Sunday school). Hannah and her sister Martha (Patty) stayed quite busy looking for a suitable building for the school and a house for the schoolmistress. When the house for the schoolmistress was finally found and the barn for the school secured, they opened their first school in 1789. They also encouraged community efforts that would build a village oven for baking bread and puddings (thus saving fuel). With this first Sunday school model in place, the More sisters promoted and administered schools in a number of other villages with much of the funding coming from members of the Clapham Sect.

Hannah insisted that there be a moral purpose in all that she taught. The object of the schools was to make honest and virtuous citizens, and this was furthered by her various savings societies. All the members, especially the women, at each meeting were encouraged to deposit a little, even a penny a week, against the rainy day. This was a type of insurance policy from which a contributor could draw from in the event of illness. This rainy day fund could even be used for maternity grants and were parceled out in monetary amounts depending on the illness and how long one would be out of commission. In an effort to stem the tide of girls found indulging in "gross living," she ordered that they were to be shunned and excluded, refusing the non-virtuous girls membership in the schools. Perhaps it sounds harsh, but Hannah was intent on raising the moral standards in the village, and this was one way to do it.

Make no doubt about the effectiveness of Hannah's work in organizing the Sunday schools for the poor. She was creatively organized and all the programs she developed were keenly devised in an effort to engage and challenge her students. She attempted to make school sessions as entertaining as possible, advising singing as one method to avert declining energy and waning attention. The lessons had to be planned and constructed to the level of the student as much as possible. She also insisted on variety to help keep the interest high and the return rate of students successful.

As far as her smallest charges were concerned, she considered kindness to be the best method in reaching children, arguing that it was possible to get the best out of them in this manner. Hannah strongly believed that terrorizing little ones did not pay, however she still believed that it was a "fundamental error to consider children as innocent beings." They were instead beings of "a corrupt nature and evil dispositions." She was not above resorting to bribery:

> "I encourage them by little bribes of a penny a chapter to get by heart certain fundamental parts of Scripture. Those who attend four Sundays without intermission receive a penny. Once in every six to eight weeks I give a little gingerbread. Once a year I distribute little books according to merit. Those who deserve most get a Bible. Second-rate merit gets a Prayer-book, the rest, cheap Repository tract."

Do you find this all rather refreshing? Instead of handing out awards to every child for work not done, only those who did the hard work were rewarded accordingly. Perhaps this is a lesson for all of our school systems and for those of us who have been parents or are parenting now.

Hannah More's Sunday school methods did find an echo among many other evangelicals. The combined methods of the More sisters and those of Robert Raikes led to the formation, in 1785, of a non-denominational national organization, The Sunday School Society. This organization's ability to coordinate and develop the work begun by Hannah More led to the amazing growth of Sunday schooling in the nineteenth century.

One of the most startling and encouraging findings by Kenneth Levine came from his study of the period around the time Hannah More was active in her Sunday schools. He noted that there were significant shifts in the working class people, elevating their status because of their increased regimes of piety, discipline and obedience in all areas of society. Not bad for a woman evangelist with a definitive calling to educate the poor in Christianity and self worth.

The More sisters had lived extraordinary lives, growing up together, working together, and living together until their deaths. They had lived out their lives at Barley Wood in the Mendip Hills until the death of Mary in 1813. It wasn't long after that the other sisters died. By 1819 Hannah was alone, suffering in poor health for a number of years. Rarely venturing past her bedroom walls, she endured a number of deathbed scenes until finally friends convinced her to move closer to them, so they could look after her a bit. Her new home was in Windsor Terrace, Clifton, and much of her time was spent in correspondence with people who had discovered her vast work in formulating Sunday schools for the poor.

When she began to sense that she was growing weaker and death was not far from her door, she began to dispense of her wealth among various charities and religious societies. Upon her death on September 7, 1833, she was buried in Wrington churchyard with her beloved sisters.

Hannah More may have been a controversial figure, but she was one of the most influential women to have achieved recognition for her work in writing tracts for the poor. Her development of Sunday schooling with her sister Martha placed her in the annals of history and Christendom as a model of what one woman can do to implement change for the betterment of the world.

As a philanthropist she was the most well known of her day and as Bebbington has commented, "In an age when avenues into any sphere outside the home were being closed, Christian zeal brought them into prominence." Christian zeal, indeed, through one Hannah More! A heart won for Christ propelled Hannah More to give her entire being for the sake of the Gospel of Christ.

Hannah More's "delicate and high-strung" personality and her fleeting dalliance with social slothfulness were ultimately overcome and used by God to minister to those who suffered physically, mentally and spiritually. Do you see that sense of purpose and direction brought godly healing into Hannah's otherwise selfish and wasted life?

To love those that society would shun, to give hope to the hopeless and to offer a moral compass to those lost, adrift in the sea of life without a rudder. This was a life spent in the service of Christ.

Scripture Application

> "COMFORT, COMFORT MY
> PEOPLE," SAYS YOUR GOD.
>
> ISAIAH 40:1

Reflections on Faith in Service to Others

When we have suffered it helps us understand another's pain. Have you undergone difficult circumstances in your life that might be used to comfort another?

It is when we take our eyes off of self that we become more content and useful in the kingdom of God. If you realize that your life is not all about "self" but rather about serving and loving the hurting people of the world, who can you reach out to today?

Embrace your purpose and destiny and experience the joy that passes all understanding. Pray for God's guidance today about His purpose for you and where He would have you serve.

In the Garden: Final Reflections

As you have encountered these women of faith and considered all that they have done in God's "Gardens of Grace," have you thought about your own work in the garden?

Have you realized God's calling for your lifetime? Are you unsure, unsteady in understanding his purpose for you? Reach out to Him and find out where He is moving and go there. Don't wait for the calling, but step out in action and run faithfully with Jesus Christ in what He is doing in the world. Don't delay. Don't worry that you won't know what to do. Remember He has equipped you uniquely for such a time as this to know your purpose. Ready? Set. Go!

Now that you are moving in faith there is just one more question I have for you: What type of flower are you in God's "Gardens of Grace?" If you are not sure, just ask a friend or loved one. I'm sure they have a very clear idea of the flower that you are in the garden. Have fun! There is no right or wrong answer. Better yet, prayerfully ask the Father and see what He has to say in regard to what flower you might be. After all He has created you uniquely and placed you perfectly in His "Gardens of Grace." God bless you as you walk in the world as a "Woman of Faith."

About the Author

Besides being a chaplain for the Arizona State Legislature, Donna Kafer is also a speaker, author and encourager in the Lord Jesus Christ. If you would like her to speak at your church, women's retreat or other event, you can contact her via her website at www.donnakafer.org or write to her at 20165 N. 67th Ave. #122-127 Glendale, AZ 85382

$\mathcal{R}$esources

Mary, Mother of Jesus

Holy Bible, New International Version
Matthew 1:18-23, Luke 1:26-56, Luke 2:1-52, John 2:1-11, John 19:25-26, Acts 1:14

Monica, Mother of St. Augustine

www.catholic.org
www.augnet.org
www.newadvent.org

Irena Sendler

Chesnoff, Richard Z. "The Other Schindlers," *US News and World Report*, March 13, 1994.
The official website of Irena Sendler: www.irenasendler.org

Margaret Beaufort

Luminarium Encyclopedia, www.luminauium.org
www.catholicity.com
www.tudorhistory.org

Susannah Wesley

www.paulbarker.org
www.historyswomen.com
www.seekinggod.org
Wesley, Foundry Pictures film, 2007, release date, 2008

Catherine Booth

www.salvationarmy.org
www.spartacusschoolnet.com
www.womenshistory.com
www.britannica.com

Blandina

Eusebius, History of the Church (*Historia Ecclesiastica*), Book V.
Chapter I.
www.catholic.org

Perpetua and Felicitas

www.catholic.org

The Two Margarets

www.applesofgold.com
www.forgodandulster.com
www.youtube.com/watch
www.scotland.org

Joan of Arc

www.distinguishedwomen.com
www.newadvent.org
www.historyguide.org/ancient/joan.html

Sophie Scholl

www.rauolwallenberg.net
www.jlrweb.com/whiterose
Sophie Scholl: The Final Days, 2005, Goldkind Filmproduktions,
Feature Film

Saint Therese of Lisieux

Therese, The Story of Saint Therese of Lisieux. Luke Films, 2005.
www.catholic.org
www.littleflower.org
www.newadvent.org
www.britannica.com
www.saint-therese.org

Hildegard von Bingen

www.who2.com/hildegardvonbingen.html
www.hildegard.org
www.infoplease.com

Phillis Wheatley

www.earlyamerica.com
www.schoolnet.com
www.historyswomen.com

Charlotte Elliott

www.cyberhymnal.org
Christian History Institute www.chigospel.com.net

Sarah Josepha Hale

www.womenwriters.com
www.bestyears.com
www.britannica.com

Hannah More

Christian History Institute – www.chigospel.org
www.gospelcom.org
www.truthandtidings.com